£15·95

HOME VIDEO: PRODUCING FOR THE HOME MARKET

by Michael Wiese

D1997794

Published by Michael Wiese Film/Video, Box 406, Westport, CT 06881, (203) 226-6979, in conjunction with Focal Press, a division of Butterworth Publishers, 80 Montvale Avenue, Stoneham, MA 02180, (617) 438-8464.

Cover and book design by Joe Feigenbaum
Back cover photograph by Nancy Wayman

Printed by Braun-Brumfield, Ann Arbor, Michigan
Manufactured in the United States of America

Copyright © 1986 by Michael Wiese
First Printing, August 1986

All rights reserved. No part of this book may be reproduced in any form or by any means without permission in writing from the author, except for the inclusion of brief quotations in a review.

This book serves as a companion to Wiese's books, **THE INDEPENDENT FILM AND VIDEOMAKERS GUIDE** and **FILM AND VIDEO BUDGETS.**

Library of Congress Catalog Card Number: 86-90135

ISBN 0-941188-04-3

Books by MICHAEL WIESE

The Independent Film & Videomakers Guide
Film & Video Budgets

*To Helen and Bill Wiese, my folks,
who advised me early on to do
whatever made me happy.
I did and I am. I thank them for that
foundation.*

TABLE OF CONTENTS

TABLE OF CONTENTS

Getting Started

Opportunities for Independents

Genres of Original Programming

Successful Video Programs

Pre-Production

Financing

The Contract

Self-Distribution

Marketing

Sales and Marketing

Packaging

Press and Publicity

Income Projections

The Future

Appendix

ACKNOWLEDGMENTS

This is my third book on film/video. The ideas expressed within come from interacting with hundreds of people: film and video producers, distributors, promoters, publicists, agents, trade and consumer press, friends and associates. The contents come from my experiences with others—their insight gathered from conversation, our hard work together, and their encouragement. I'd like to thank those who've helped and participated with me.

First Morgan, my wife. She has given up weekends, vacation days and many evenings together so that I can write. She knows when a book (or video project) is bubbling inside even when I don't. When I stammer and plead that, *"this project really won't take too long,"* she knows better. Nevertheless she has supported me and kept me on track in this and every other project, book or event I've produced. Now after more than 2 1/2 years, she can see this book in print. She knows and understands my peculiar process—that only after I clear out the information in my head through writing can I go on to other areas of exploration. She shares with me in the credit when I say *"we did it."* Thank you, Morgan, for your insights and partnership in balancing our marriage, a full-time job and a cottage book industry.

Secondly, I must salute Austin Furst, friend, mentor, boss, chairman and founder of *Vestron Video*. He offered me my present job as Vice President of Program Development and allowed me to explore with him in home video's most exciting years. He is the best programmer and video entrepreneur I've ever met. He has challenged me into finding new avenues of programming that I doubt I would have on my own.

Jon Peisinger, Vestron's President has created a place where miracles happen. He has developed a creative environment of spontaneous cooperation, where programming and marketing people have achieved unprecedented success in the country's most competitive business. Here, he has offered me the chance, and challenge, to develop and produce the widest range of programming available anywhere. He has guided me through numerous tough and risky decisions. He generously shared the position as Co-Executive Producer with me on Vestron's first feature film, *The Beach Boys: An American Band*, and advised me in my biggest project of 1986, the *National Geographic* Video series. He has been the best boss I've ever had, sharing with me his hard-earned knowledge of home video and keeping my plate filled with new challenges.

Without the support and opportunities that Austin and Jon provided me this book would be a pamphlet.

My friends and associates at Vestron have also acted as extensions in my education, leading me into new areas, coming up with ideas for programming, and often challenging the premise for creating programs. Is it a good idea? Will it sell? How can we market it? Without this daily interaction, few of the ideas in this book would have matured. I would especially like to thank my staff, Melissa Hoffman, Jeffrey Peisch, Kathy Gould, Lisa Aquirre, Chris Cisero, Sally Jobson, and Larry Kasanoff (now with the feature film department) for joining me 150% in the challenge of creating, developing and producing for home video.

This book began in 1983 when I left *Showtime/The Movie Channel*—before I joined Vestron. The heat was off pay TV. Home video was the new buzz word.

I told Arlyn Powell, editor at *Focal Press/Butterworth*, about my idea for a book on home video. He liked it immediately and offered to co-publish it as he had done with my first two books. Without the confidence that this relationship gave me, it would have been very difficult to proceed. His patience and overall support during the last few years continues to be greatly appreciated.

A boost toward productivity also came from Ellen Lazer, and Barbara Miller of Knowledge Industry Publications who asked me to write the chapter *"How a Video Program Is Made"* for *Guide to Videotape Publishing* (ISBN 086729-167-2). They graciously allowed me to use what I wrote within this book.

Simultaneously, my seminars, *Independent Film and Video: Financing and Marketing Techniques* for the *American Film Institute*, keep me in close touch with hundreds of independent producers throughout the country. The seminars and my day-to-day interaction with producers at Vestron give me a focus for this book. I talk to the producers about their problems and this exchange has led me to find creative solutions and insights to share. My thanks go to Emily Laskin, Director of National Educational Programs, and her staff at the AFI for giving me the platform to present my ideas.

This book was supposed to be easy to produce. I would dictate the book onto tape; these would be transcribed directly onto word processing disks. The disks would be reworked and revised, and then telecommunicated to the printer for typesetting. Easy to say—hard to do.

Joan Hoffman, an educator in computer literacy, graciously struggled through my dictation tapes, and learned, at my request, an antiquated word processing program that worked on my old Apple II + . She shared new programs and computer techniques that improved our working system. My thanks go to her for suggestions and help in refining this process and for making my job much easier.

I'm also appreciative of Marcia Clark, a professional copy editor and proofreader who helped me make sense.

Joe Feigenbaum cracked the bat for a home run with his text and cover design. He designed my first two books as well. I'm proud of how good they look.

Nancy Wayman, a professional photographer, friend and neighbor, shot the back cover photo and made the author look like someone I'd like to meet. Thank you, Nancy.

Again, my appreciation goes out to the composition department at *Braun-Brumfield*, especially Barbara Wasneski and Barbara Burns and to Mary Murrel, my account manager, who kept the job moving.

Thanks, also, to Dick Bunnell of New England Book Components who oversaw the printing of the book's cover.

PERMISSIONS AND CREDITS

And thanks to the many manufacturers and video publishers who very generously allowed me to share with you examples of their cassette packaging and promotion.

I had hoped to assemble packaging examples from all the major video publishers. Some did not respond to requests for art work. To those that did, I am very grateful. I also wish to thank the researchers whose data has been included in the charts.

Cassette boxes for *Making Michael Jackson's Thriller, Halley's Comet* (Japanese version), *Truly Tasteless Jokes, Father Guido Sarducci Goes to College, Whoopi Goldberg, Joe Piscopo, Women Tell The Dirtiest Jokes, Richard Pryor: Live and Smokin', Hooker, National Geographic Video (The Sharks and Land of the Tiger), 20-Minute Workout, The Secret World of Erotic Art, Armed Forces Workout, Breaking with the Mighty Poppalots, Treasure, The Care Bears Movie, Pete Townshend: White City, Liberace Live, Cat On A Hot Tin Roof, Lords of the Ring* (Japanese version), *Ringmasters: The Great American Bash, The Winning Edge* with John McEnroe and Ivan Lendl, *Weight Watchers Magazine Guide To A Healthy Lifestyle, Weight Watchers Magazine Guide to Dining and Cooking, Comedy Videos, Dick Clark's Best of Bandstand, Steve Martin Live, New Wave Comedy, Bette Midler: Art or Bust, Penthouse Video: Love Stories, The Statue of Liberty and Academy Award Winners: Animated Short Films* and one sheets for

The Beach Boys: An American Band, Lisa Sliwa's Common Sense Defense, The Prince and Princess of Wales: Talking Personally, and *National Geographic Video* courtesy of Vestron Video.

Cassette boxes for *Debbie Does Las Vegas, The Police Tapes,* and *The Best Legs in the Eighth Grade* courtesy of Lightning Video.

Cassette boxes for *The Little Prince, Challenge of the Gobots* (Vol. 4), and *Benji,* courtesy of Children's Video Library.

Cassette boxes for *Eat To Win, Jane Fonda's New Workout,* and *Jane Fonda's Prime Time Workout* courtesy of Karl Video or Karl/Lorimar Home Video.

Cassette boxes for *The Compleat Beatles* and *The Joy of Stocks* courtesy of MGM/UA Video, copyright 1982 and 1984 respectively.

Cassette boxes for *Baseball: The Pete Rose Way,* and *The Love Goddesses* courtesy of Embassy Home Entertainment.

Cassette boxes for *Raquel: Total Beauty* and *Fitness and The World At War* (Vol. 20) courtesy of Thorn EMI Video.

Cassette boxes for *Hardware Wars* courtesy of Ernie Fosselius/Michael Wiese and Warner Home Video.

Cassette box for *Bayou Romance* courtesy Prism Entertainment.

Charts *''Projected Growth in VCR Sales and Pre-Recorded Videocassette Sales''* courtesy of Video Marketing Newsletter.

Chart *''Top 10 Selling Exercise Tapes''* courtesy of Knowledge Industry Publications.

Chart *''Percentage-of-Revenue Sources''*, and *''Retail Sales to Rentals''* courtesy of Merrill Lynch.

Chart *''Film Producer Revenues''* courtesy of Wilkofsky-Gruen/Merrill Lynch.

Chart *"Programming Mix 1985 and 1995"* is combined from data from Gallup Reports and Wilkofsky-Gruen respectively.

Charts *"Market Share Survey of Video Software Suppliers and Company Rankings"* reprinted with permission of Home Viewer/Video Week Trendicator Reports.Copyright 1986. All rights reserved.

Chart *"Video Retailer Purchase by Genre"* courtesy of Video Software Dealers Association (VSDA).

FOREWORD

A Time to Begin

Financing and marketing a videotape is often more difficult than actually producing the tape. At various times, I have found myself on both sides of the desk—first as a seller, an independent producer; and now as a buyer, a developer of original video programs for a distributor. Having gained experience in two very different areas, I shall do my best to steer producers in directions that will save time, money and unnecessary effort.

This book will explore program forms and genres, the inner workings of distribution deals, and the ways in which original videotape programs are marketed. Today's hits may quickly be replaced by new ones, but the principles covered in this book on producing, distributing and marketing videotapes will hopefully hold up for some time.

Home video is exciting. It is only in its infancy. Like the blue-sky days of pay TV, home video will have its own successes and failures. Producers must be very selective in developing ideas that are appropriate for the marketplace.

New forms can be explored, but cautiously. Producers need to develop an understanding of the market before allowing themselves to be seduced by their own brilliant ideas. As an independent producer, I have two file cabinets crammed full of projects that I'd like to do. Because they are *''significant,''* and *''meaningful,''* they are of great personal interest to me. But right now I couldn't even sell them to myself. The distribution channels are still emerging. Many are too small for some of these programs.

To understand the market, study home video successes and their audiences. You will quickly recognize why those ideas worked. Discover ideas and opportunities that appeal to you and to an audience before beginning production.

Producers' and distributors' viewpoints are often very different. A producer is challenged by making programs in which he or she finds personal interest. Fine. After all, who would want to spend six months to a year or more writing, producing and editing a program if he or she has no heart for it? A distributor's viewpoint is markedly different. *Can the program be sold? To whom?* Most producers don't consider that distributors ask these questions of program submissions every day. Distributors don't want to try something new. They want to do what works (sells).

The traditional video business consists of manufacturers using wholesalers to supply a video retail *''rental pool''* with home videocassettes. Therefore, in actuality, it is the wholesaler and the retailer, not the consumer, who is the buyer for most tapes. (This is changing somewhat as new distribution channels emerge.) Most producers haven't thought about this one simple—and quite important—fact: The tape must interest a retailer to make the tape successful.

Retailers, the real customers, are not sophisticated movie or TV people. They recognize hit films like *Ghostbusters, Rambo*, or *Rocky* and stars like Clint Eastwood and Burt Reynolds, but when you start moving away from *''A''* titles into original programs, the retailer's attention span and interest diminish. It then becomes the distributor's job to pitch other program forms and the producer's job to deliver something to which the retailer will respond. If the retailer doesn't recognize it, he won't buy it, and the public will never see it.

The consumer too must recognize the program. Most people who own videotape machines *''time-shift''*—that is, record and later play back their favorite television shows. Fewer people rent prerecorded videotapes. Fewer, still, buy tapes. Once people have rented feature films, and learn that there are other forms of programming, they may begin to seek them out. As of this writing, there are enough people just beginning to do this, that it is feasible to produce some original programs for home video. These programs can be exercise, instructional, documentary, lifestyle, music, comedy and so on.

Producers may want to set aside their own impassioned desire to produce, and for a moment get into the heads of distributors, retailers and consumers. It is illuminating and ultimately rewarding to give up preconceptions about a specific program and see how the buyers may respond. This exercise will provide a greater understanding of how tapes are marketed, distributed and eventually used. Your insight will pay dividends later.

Some Biographical Background

The process and conclusions I am about to describe are not based on research or theory but have developed from the film and video experience I've had, from the hits and the misses.

When I started, I made many films: documentaries, biographies, sports, art, performance, music, spiritual, wildlife, personal, experimental and comedy. I never paid any attention to how they would be promoted or sold. I figured that if my films were well written, acted, shot, and edited, and if the music was good and the subject matter meaningful, moving or inspiring, the films would somehow sell themselves. Well, it doesn't quite work that way. Most of these projects brought in numerous awards, but numerous dollars didn't automatically follow.

The financing for most of my films came from private investors, people who expected the films to make money. (The process of fundraising is described in detail in my first book, *The Independent Film and Videomakers Guide*.) I hoped to develop a string of money-making films and to expand my group of happy investors. Since most of my films were not money-makers and were not marketed, I lost my ability (and the confidence) to raise money. After 15 years of working independently I had to try something new.

I got a job. The first was as a segment producer for a San Francisco television station—writing and producing segments for a talk, variety, entertainment show. The segments were mostly fluff. (I'd occasionally try to book *''meaningful people''* but by the time the host got through with them, they had lost all opportunity to ''make a statement.'')

I finally learned. The show was not the time or place. The purpose of the show was to entertain and to get ratings. I quickly learned that if I did segments that were promotable in *TV Guide*—with sex, food or baby animals—we'd get good ratings. I learned a great deal about prime-time programming. The show had goals other than those I held as an independent filmmaker. The programming held no deep personal interest. Everything I produced didn't have to make a statement. In fact, the station executives preferred it didn't! So, instead of doing something culturally significant I simply tried to produce segments that could be fun. There were segments on anything from *Termite Sniffing Dogs* to *Tot Wrestlers*, from *The Beverly Hills Diet* to the *Ms. Nude America Pageant*.

Next I moved to New York as head of production for an agency that produces political campaigns. In less than a year I oversaw the production of 175 television spots for 18 gubernatorial and senatorial campaigns, 60 radio spots, two sponsored films and a documentary. The goal was simple—get votes. Not to entertain, not to enlighten, not to inform—but to create a presence for the candidate. It was a marketing game of matching personalities with public issues—to win votes.

Later, I was director of on-air production and promotion for *Showtime/The Movie Channel*. Here the audience was the pay-TV subscriber. Without subscriber *''satisfaction''* (a pay-television market research term), he or she would disconnect and the network would lose revenue. The purpose of the *''interstitial''* programs (which aired between the movies) that my department produced was to hold onto the subscriber. Our job was to create a network identity through appealing graphics and segments that promoted the network as having *''more movies, the best movies, 24 hours a day,''* thereby differentiating us from the competition (HBO). Soft-sell star profile segments used actors and directors who'd talk about their upcoming movies on the network. There were contests and special promotions to keep the subscribers involved, tuned in and paying their monthly bills.

In a few short years I learned that there are many reasons to produce programs other than self-discovery and personal growth. The new kinds of programs I produced had an intended result—to gain ratings, win votes, keep subscribers. In each case, my job as a producer was to satisfy a specific purpose. As an independent producer my focus had always been on pleasing myself, creating a meaningful program.

In my last two jobs, I was personally responsible for the budgets. I spent millions of dollars on production and this gave me a tremendous opportunity to learn, to experiment with new techniques in film and video. By my calculations it would have taken me 10 years to spend that much money as an independent producer.

As of this writing, I am Vice-President of Program Development at Vestron Video. Vestron is the largest independent videotape distributor in the world, serving 31 countries. Vestron is in the packaged goods business; it sells videocassettes. My staff can develop and produce anything it wants—as long as it sells. This rare opportunity has given me a chance to produce a great variety of original program forms and to see directly the importance of marketing.

I work with dozens of outside producers on new video programs. Together we twist and turn ideas into marketable programs for home video. In any one week my department will evaluate 100 projects, oversee 25 in production, and another 50 in development. In 1986 Vestron will release 55 to 70 original programs. Fortunately, the video business has been very healthy, and every original program we've released has shown a profit. This points to the importance of selecting the right projects as every one represents an opportunity to lose money!

For each success, there are more than a hundred proposals that we do not distribute. A portion may be distributed by others. Most fail because producers haven't taken the time to understand the marketplace. They lack knowledge in packaging, in marketing, in promotion. I stood in their shoes not too long ago.

During the last five years, I've been a national seminar leader on film and video financing, production and distribution for *The American Film Institute*. I do this for two reasons. First, to assist new producers in their work. And secondly, to stay close to the creative community. I've had the opportunity to speak with thousands of producers about their projects. Most are bright, creative people, enthusiastic about their ideas. However, many of their projects will fail because they aren't thinking about how the marketplace works when they set out to produce. That's what I hope to clarify in this book, as well as program development, production and distribution. Hopefully, through this book, producers can knock years (and thousands of dollars of failures) off an otherwise long and frustrating path.

Now, having been on both sides of the distributor's desk, my task is to take producers through the step-by-step process of developing and producing successful home video programs. I'll do my best to present the many opportunities that exist in home video. Enjoy the book. Let it spark your imagination and benefit your projects.

And may all your videos be certified ''*gold*.''

Best wishes,

Michael Wiese
Westport, Connecticut
August 1986

THE EMERGENCE OF HOME VIDEO

The Emergence of Home Video

"People began to imagine the possibilities . . . they began to program themselves."

The Emergence of Home Video

In order to know where the new video revolution may be going, a brief journey from its roots might prove useful.

Home video began with hardware when Sony introduced the first Betamax video recorder in 1975. It was priced high ($1,300) and could only record one hour per tape. The video disc player emerged as the only hardware competitor. There were two: the laser disc from MCA and a capacitance disc (CED) from RCA, both which retailed between $500 and $1,000. The Betamax could record off the air and be used for time-shifting; the disc formats were playback only. Most people figured that the discs, because they were cheaper to buy, would win the hardware war. (This was not to be the case.)

A few years later the VHS format was created. With several non-compatible hardware systems, potential buyers were confused. No one wanted to end up with an obsolete format. Should they buy Beta (good quality, short tape running time) or VHS (lesser quality, longer tape running time) or one of the two disc format players (high quality, cheap, but no recording capability)?

Although the VHS recorder did produce recordings of a slightly inferior quality when compared to Beta, it could record two hours, twice as much as Beta. This one factor probably won people over to the VHS format. Soon thereafter VHS extended recording time to four then six hours. Beta extended to two hours. Most people who time-shift were attracted to the longer tapes, both for convenience and economy. This popularized VHS so that today the formats are split 85% VHS/ 15% BETA with the latter continuing to lose ground. (Today, many video retailers do not even stock Beta tapes.)

In home video's early days the primary use of VCRs was to record favorite programs off the air for playback later. This quasi-illegal vicarious thrill was given further boost when in 1984 (after a previous lower court decision in 1981), the Supreme Court reversed the decision so that private off-airing taping was not in violation of the copyright laws. This verdict helped propel the video revolution. People began to imagine the possibilities. They could watch TV when they wanted to watch—which was not necessarily when something was aired. They were beginning to act as their own programmers.

Early on, other than X-rated films on video, there was little available. Even X-rated tapes sold for as much as $125. Early prerecorded cassettes of movies sold for $80. Blank tape costs were also high. Nevertheless, the first attempts at marketing videotapes for sale were through direct mail. Both Time-Life and CBS Video Club tried. Both failed. Unfortunately there were too few VCR owners and too much expense involved in reaching potential purchasers. Fotomat and others tried rental methods by mail, which also failed.

The movie studios really did not see videotapes as more than a small anxiliary market. If they had they would have grabbed control early on and prevented Andre Blay from creating Magnetic Video, which he did by purchasing the rights to some 50 20th Century Fox films for a pittance. (Fox later bought back the company for $7.2 million to begin CBS/Fox Video.) In a move that is now legend, Austin Furst licensed the video rights to Time-Life's video inventory when the company left the video business and founded Vestron Video, now the second largest of U.S. video publishers.

In the late '70s, no one could have imagined that by 1986 home video revenues would nearly equal that of box office receipts and that by 1990 box office revenues would be significantly junior to home video!

Many things changed to bring this about. In the early days raw videotape and duplication costs were still high and so were retail prices. These high prices kept people from buying tapes and spurred on the growth of the rental market. Most studios hated the rental business because it deprived them from controlling their income and earning income on every rental. Warner Home Video, in an early effort to gain control, instituted a complex rental plan with video merchants so they would share in every video rental. (Other studios, MGM/UA and CBS/Fox, also had similar plans.) Retailers balked and there was significant backlash. Not only were the plans logistically unworkable but the retailers and wholesalers already had a taste of this new business and collectively liked things just the way they were. They were not interested in sharing rental income: period. They were willing to pay high prices for programs but wanted the subsequent income they themselves generated through rentals.

The reason retailers could keep money on rentals stemmed from the First Sale doctrine that says that anyone may purchase a copyrighted tape and then rent the tape to others without having to pay any more to the copyright owner. All the money from tape rentals can go straight into a video retailer's pocket. Of course this ruling, to this day, drives the Hollywood studios and copyright owners out of their minds. In every other licensing area they are used to receiving and controlling income. For years the Hollywood studios lobbied Congress to pass legislation repealing or abolishing the First Sale doctrine so that they could be compensated for the lost income that video retailers have been collecting. Various means of compensating the copyright owners have been proposed—such as taxing prerecorded and blank tapes and putting a surcharge on video recorder sales. None of these plans has passed Congress. The Hollywood studios have argued that videotape prices for movies have been artificially high ($79) in order to ensure their own profits and that if the doctrine were abolished, they could then drop prices, and create a much larger *"sell-through market."*

The video retailers on the other hand feel that the system works fine as it is. *"If it ain't broken, don't try to fix it."* Retailers are accustomed to renting tapes at low prices ($1-$6). They argue that if they had to pay a percentage of each rental to the studios then they would have to increase the rental prices which in turn would diminish rentals and thwart the growth of consumers' fascination with renting.

So far, it looks like the First Sale doctrine will stay. With every passing day and the phenomenal monies generated by video rentals and sales, the studios' argument that they are losing money is lessened in the eyes of Congress and everyone concerned.

In 1978 there were a little more than half a million VCR machines in place. The next year the number doubled to over a million. The next year, it doubled again. By the end of 1985 it hit nearly 30 million machines in the U.S., and 100 million VCRs worldwide. In 1986 through 1988 it is expected that 10-13 million machines per year will be sold. Back in 1978 there were about 1.3 million prerecorded cassettes sold. By 1984 there were nearly 22 million sold; in 1985 this number more than doubled to 56 million. This year it is expected that 65-70 million will be sold.

On the marketing end there was an explosion of large and small video publishers entering the marketplace. The major studios (Paramount, CBS/Fox, Disney, MCA, RCA/Columbia, and Warners) had home video divisions. Independents like Karl Video (now Karl-Lorimar Video) and Vestron were created by entrepreneurial visionaries. Today, there are 10 video publishers that control 85% of the marketplace, and another 250 video publishers that share the remaining 15%.

Videos were first rented (hardly ever sold) through video specialty retail shops, the *"mom and pops."* Former plumbers, soft-ice cream makers and local entrepreneurs opened video rental stores in storefronts throughout the land. Today there are 25,000 retail outlets. Besides these outlets, record stores, bookstores, toy stores and discount chains sell videotapes today. Other outlets that rent tapes include convenience, drug and grocery stores.

Today VCR owners use their machines so much that pay and network television systems as well as movie theaters are experiencing a diminished viewership. People are staying home and watching videotapes. *The convenience and economy of home video has made it the primary means for viewing movies!*

In a flash, home video has exploded into a multibillion dollar industry. Few could have predicted its haphazard and unplanned growth. Video seemingly has come out of nowhere and has changed the way we view programs. Even today few people really understand what makes it work or why people are so attracted to it. This aspect alone has made investors wary. Is this another American fad? Will it fizzle out like 8-track tapes or video games? Probably not. There are already too many machines in place. The VCR has become a permanent appliance in the home. However, in an industry so volatile, there will certainly be many shakeouts as the market matures. Those producers, distributors and retailers who are mindful of the marketplace will survive. Many will fail.

The good news for producers is that more than two-thirds of the films in the studio vaults (the better films) have already been released. Consequently the hunger for new product will be difficult to feed without new programming of all kinds. There is still plenty of time for innovative producers and programmers to develop and produce the future hits of tomorrow.

The purpose of this book is to prepare producers for entry in this new world of original programming. Fasten your seatbelts.

INTRODUCTION

Introduction

''There is every indication that as viewers gobble up more video they will seek out other forms of programming.''

Introduction

With the tremendous penetration of videotape players into U.S. households, there is every indication that as viewers gobble up more and more feature films on video they will begin to seek out other kinds of programming. Attention has already turned to non-feature programs with music, such as *Making Michael Jackson's Thriller* (Vestron Video, 1983), exercise programs such as *The Jane Fonda Workout* (Karl Video, 1983), diet programs such as *Eat To Win* (Karl/Lorimar, 1985) and comedy programs such as *Gallagher* (Paramount, 1984). These non-feature film genres point the way to new opportunities for producers, distributors and consumers for the creation and use of new forms of entertainment and education.

Along with the development of new programming forms, new outlets for videotapes are emerging, from the video specialty rental store to bookstores, drugstores, convenience and grocery stores, sports outlets and toy stores. Videotapes are sold by such mass merchandisers as K mart, Penney's and Target Stores. Magazines and direct marketing advertisements offer up your favorite videotapes for sale by mail and phone. Efforts to sell videotapes on television are also under way.

Now is the time for innovative producers to study the new programming

MAKING
MICHAEL JACKSON'S
THRILLER
STEREO
Including
"MICHAEL JACKSON'S THRILLER"
a short film directed by
JOHN LANDIS

forms and marketing opportunities for this new medium of amusement and education.

MARKET ORIENTATION

Shocking Facts

Where do the ideas for new programs come from? How are they produced? How and where are they sold? What makes one tape successful and another a flop? How is a tape marketed? Let's look first at some facts that may upset the applecart.

Shocking Fact One: The most important step in creating a videotape program is not the idea. That comes later. First, you must be very clear on the category of your program. What exactly is it? Not *"It's sort of like this and a little like this,"* but exactly what is it? It's a big name stand-up comedy show. It's a rock and roll documentary. It's an aerobics tape for women. If you say, *"It's a play in which Hungarian child actors and their mothers talk about physics in while woodworking and it's edited like a music video with fast cuts and Swedish,"* then you can expect to be misunderstood in the marketplace.

Once you've answered *"What is it?"* you're ready to ask the Big Question: *"Is there a market for this tape?"* This is what you must find out before magnetic tape passes over the recording heads. I think our first three examples (comedy, music, exercise) were very clear. You knew what they were. You could say *"yes"* to the form without losing sleep. The Hungarian woodcarving music video is so convoluted in form it would take a rocket scientist to figure out what it is and an Iacocca to sell it.

Too many producers are seduced by their own brilliant ideas. They need to understand first how the tape will be sold and later used. The original program department at Vestron reviews 100 programs, proposals, rough cuts, and finished videos every week. (That's a healthy sign of the creative community at work.) What's upsetting is the volume of projects in which the creator has no idea how the project will be sold. It's an easy trap to fall into. You have an idea, you scurry off to produce your vision, but you neglect to understand the market environment enough to determine whether your idea is worth anything to anyone. Why would someone want to buy it?

So many proposals come in with a paragraph or two about the *"videotape revolution."* None fails to mention that *"there are tens of millions of video machines in the U.S. alone."* The proposal writers try to convince me of the value of their videotape by stating boldly, *"If only 1% of the people who own the machines buy the tape, we'll all be millionaires."* They expect a check by return mail.

These proposal writers stopped probing too soon. Too little market research can be deadly. What they failed to recognize is that most videotapes are sold not to consumers but to video stores, which in turn mostly rent these tapes to consumers. Their model for millions is quickly shattered.

Shocking Fact Two: The traditional videotape business is, at present, primarily a rental market. Therefore, the market for most tapes is the nation's 20,000 video rental stores—the mom and pop rental store—not the millions of people with machines. The retailers are the primary customers. They're the ones who will buy the tape and in turn, rent it out! Not understanding this one fact alone has led hundreds of producers down the path to ruin. They based their income projections on millions rather than thousands of potential customers.

Shocking Fact Three: To make matters worse, these individual stores are besieged by wholesalers who want to sell 400 to 500 different titles each and every month! The retailer is overwhelmed. He may buy the 20 or so *''must have''* hit titles that he knows he can rent—the *Rambos*, the *Ghostbusters*, the *48 Hours*. Then, if his cash flow is strong from the previous month, he may pick some *''B''* titles. If he's really feeling adventuresome, the wholesaler may convince him to pick *''C''* and *''D''* titles. Or maybe he'll never look that far. And this is where most original programs are hidden.

Study the environment in which your videotapes will be sold. If you define as your market the video retail stores, you will quickly see that it is very difficult (but not impossible) to design non-feature programs for what is essentially a *''feature film''* environment. It can be and has been done—this is clearly the wave of the future. But one must proceed cautiously.

NEW MARKETS/NEW ORIENTATIONS

Book Based

So much for the shocking facts. Happier news is that another market is beginning to burgeon: bookstores. Waldenbooks, B. Dalton, Doubleday and others are starting to sell from 30 to 50 videotape titles in hundreds of their stores. Note the word *''sell.''* Since book retailers customarily sell books, it's no surprise that they'd look for other products—like videotapes—that they can also sell. But tapes sold in bookstores have to be *''priced to sell.''* The magic number today is under $30. Prices even go as low as $6.99.

This book-based environment requires that videotape titles have a relationship to book titles and promotable subjects that will be recognizable to bookstore retailers and customers alike. Keep this in mind when exploring possibilities for original programs. Hit titles at low prices will be an easy call for bookstore buyers. Titles like *''Raiders''*

(Paramount, 1983), *"Thriller"* (Vestron Video, 1983), *"Jane Fonda's Workout"* (Karl Video, 1983), Disney products, and black and white classic movies can be found in many bookstores.

As bookstores gain more experience with video, they will stock a greater number of different titles. It will be creative producers who can identify likely titles for these outlets. *"Weight Watcher's Guide to a Healthy Lifestyle"* (Vestron Video, 1985) was bought by the three major book chains. It makes sense—the booksellers had seen two *Weight Watcher's* books on the best-seller list. Bookstore buyers understand this kind of video product. They know what it is. They know how to sell it.

Business Oriented

Business-oriented tapes are sold into a very different marketplace altogether. In the business and industry market, training and motivational tapes and films are sold for hundreds of dollars (e.g. $500-$1,500). The programs contain very specific information on subjects such as salesmanship, time management, investment banking, Japanese business practices—information that can't be found elsewhere. Top business consultants and successful entrepreneurs are the *"stars."* These tapes are designed specifically for and are sold to the Fortune 1000 corporations that need the information and can afford the high price tag: a small market with very refined needs. If a tape sells only a few hundred copies, it can probably recoup its production cost.

Schools/Libraries

Schools and libraries are also a very specialized and diminishing market. Producers entering this field should proceed cautiously. Many are leaving this arena because there just isn't the money available for media that there used to be. Video is seen as a blessing, however, to buyers in this market who have been accustomed to paying $15-$20 per minute for 16mm film prints. The videocassette represents a low-cost alternative. Today, 80% of all public schools use videocassettes in the classroom. By next year this will increase to 90%.

If you are producing for this market, you must research the tapes and films that already exist. Learn if there is sufficient demand among educational media buyers. School and library needs are highly defined. Educational media generally follow classroom curricula. (If your program deviates significantly from course textbooks, you will lose sales.) Unlike entertainment-based traditional video markets, the educational market seeks out instructional material.

Direct Marketing

Although a very expensive way to sell videotape programs, direct marketing does enable producers with narrowly focused programs to sell directly to a target audience. A mailer for a wildlife program can be mailed directly to wildlife groups. Ads can be placed in wildlife periodicals. If you can determine who the end-users are, where they are, whether they'll buy videocassettes, and how to reach them, then direct marketing can be effective.

These are some of the markets for videotapes. Learn them. Study successful programs and their campaigns. Study the losers as well. Find out what happened. Seek out producers whose work bears some similarity to yours. Ask questions. Accumulate knowledge before you spend dollar one and you'll be ahead of the pack.

STATISTICS

Statistics

''The average customer is only in the video store for about 10 minutes.''

Home Video Statistics

Statistics are like road markers. They are like a snapshot in time on the home video highway, indicating where we've been and where we might be headed. An overview of the industry can be gleaned from this information. Keep in mind too that these statistics come from a wide variety of reporters and their snapshots represent differing points of view—some are bullish on home video, others more conservative. Consequently, in comparing these numbers you may find contradictions. But here's the big picture.

VCR Penetration

The most important indicator as to the size and growth of the market is the number of videotape machines in consumer's hand. Without a machine base, there is no market for programming. The larger the machine base, the wider variety of programming opportunities beyond movies.

Projected Growth in VCR Sales and Penetration in the U. S.

Year	**VCRs sold** (millions)	**VCR households** (millions)	**TV households** (%)
1985	11.9	25.6	29.7%
1986	12.5	36.1	41.0%
1987	10.8	44.7	49.9%
1988	9.9	51.7	56.9%
1989	9.4	57.8	62.4%
1990	9.7	63.3	67.3%

(Source: Video Marketing)

The size of the VCR universe also suggests marketing approaches. Studies show that when VCRs reach at least 30% of all TV households, direct marketing will be cost effective. We have just come to that point.

Video analysts say that when 50% of America's TV homes have videotape machines, there will be a significant expansion in original non-feature programming. Hollywood simply does not have the capacity to produce enough films for the consumer appetite. People will begin looking for other programs and new ways to use their VCRs.

Prerecorded Videocassette Sales
(all channels of distribution)

Year	**Millions of Units**	**% Change**
1980	3.0	—
1981	5.5	83.3%
1982	6.0	9.1%
1983	11.0	83.3%
1984	22.0	100.0%
1985	55.0	150.0%
1986	65.5	19.1%
1987	72.0	9.9%

(Source: Video Marketing)

Prerecorded Cassette Users

Just because someone has a VCR it doesn't mean he or she will rent or buy or even play prerecorded cassettes (PRCs). Most people use their video machines to time-shift—to record and play back TV programs later. According to a Nielsen report the proportion of VCR owners who rent has increased from about 37% in 1984 to nearly 45% in 1985. Since not everyone uses VCRs to watch prerecorded cassettes, the total machine base is not an accurate count of potential renters and purchasers of PRCs.

Sales-to-Rental Ratios

Most sales are made to video specialty stores that rent the tapes to consumers. The average store stocks about 1,500-3,000 tapes and turns 1,000 transactions per week; 98% of these are rentals. The 2% of sales represents 21% of the store's revenues. Sales are continuing to make up a larger and larger share of home video revenues.

Demographics

Who are the people who have bought VCRs? If we know something about them we may be able to discover what kind of programming appeals to them and how we might reach them. Most surveys peg the current VCR owner as well-educated, between the ages of 25 and 50, with an income between $20,000-$50,000. They are technologically savvy; they own stereos and computers. Half are women. They live in urban areas with about 25% each in four areas: the Northeast, the West, the South and the Central portion. Seventy-five percent have VHS machines. They are heavy TV watchers and use the VCR to time-shift. According to a 1985 R. H. Bruskin Associates survey, purchasers of VCRs fall into the following age groups:

VCR Purchasers

Ages	18 to 24	18%
	25 to 34	29%
	35 to 49	31%
	50 to 64	14%
	Over 65	8%

Some 60% of all owners are between the age of 25 and 49. Programming that is designed for this age group has a greater likelihood of success.

ASI Market Research recently determined that video customers are well-educated. Most have some college (52%), did post-graduate work (14%), or have finished high school (31%). The median annual income is $37,000, with 31% earning more than $50,000, and 23% earning less than $25,000. Customers are equally divided between women and men. Nearly 75% of all renters are between 25 and 49 years of age.

Of course, as machine prices fall and second machines come into the home, these demographics could even out. Note that the younger record-buying group between the ages of 12-18 is not even calculated. That tells you something right away about the recent low sales of youth-oriented music videos. This will change when teenagers have their own VCRs.

The ASI Market Research study also said that only 1% of video store customers come to buy cassettes. Seventy-four percent come to rent or return tapes and 25% to buy video-related items or browse. Most (64% of men, 57% of women) who come to a store make up their minds what to rent once they are there. Marketers thus have a tremendous opportunity to influence rental with point-of-purchase displays. However since the average customer is only in the store about 10 minutes, he or she has to do it quickly.

Cassettes Sold and Rented to Consumers

According to a 1985 Nielsen report, 74% of VCR owners have rented a prerecorded cassette at least once. Sixty-seven percent are active renters and rent at least once per month.

Tape sales will increase as prices decrease to near that of record albums or hard-cover books. Paul Kagan, publisher of *VCR Letter*, writes that as mass merchants enter the market VCR owners will be almost three times as likely to buy a cassette in 1986 as they were in 1981. Each VCR household (on the average) will account for one sale in 1986. Not every title will be collectible. Renting a tape for a few dollars per night will continue to be a great value.

Certified *"Gold"*

Remember that most tapes today are movies and are sold to the video specialty stores that rent them. Presently, if a theatrical tape sells 75,000 units or generates $3 million at retail prices then it is deemed *"gold"* by the RIAA (Recording Industry of America Association). If a theatrical tape sells 150,000 units or $6 million at retail then it is deemed *"platinum."*

If a non-theatrical tape (one that hasn't been in theatrical release)—most are non-feature programs—sells 30,000 units or $1.5 million at retail it is certified *"gold."* At 60,000 units or $2 million at retail it is *"platinum."* Note the considerable differences between theatrical and non-theatrical levels set by the RIAA. In both cases these are significant, best-seller levels, obtained by only hundreds of titles each year.

Total Home Video Revenues

According to the Fairfield Group, a market research group, the prerecorded video business is $3.3 billion in 1985 sales and rentals. This is bigger than books, about the same as pay TV and nearly equal to the record and theatrical box office revenues. Video has grown up fast. When the percentage-of-revenue sources are compared, it is projected that by 1990 home video will account for 31% and domestic theatrical box office for 23%.

	1980	1985	1990
Theatrical Total	78.5%	47.0%	38.0%
Domestic	45.8	30.0	23.0
Foreign	32.7	17.0	15.0
Cable			
Pay Channel Subscribers	5.0	16.4	19.0
Pay Per View	—	1.5	4.0
Network Television	6.3	4.3	3.0
Syndication and other TV	9.0	7.8	5.0
Home Video	1.2	23.0	31.0
Total	100.0	100.0	100.0

(Source: Merrill Lynch)

International

The world VCR population is about 100 million. Japan and the U.S. account for about half. At the end of 1985, Japan had 19 million; United Kingdom, 9 million; West Germany, nearly 7 million; France, Canada, Turkey and Australia, approximately 3 million each; Spain, 2 million; and so on. These markets also offer an opportunity for original programs to producers who understand the programming needs of each country.

According to a Mackintosh International research survey, in 1987 international VCR penetration will reach the following levels: UK, 59%; Holland, 51%; Germany, 41%; Spain, 24%; Austria, 22%; Italy, 7%. Penetration in Europe will reach 40% by 1990, 60% in the U.S., and 75% in Japan.

The European markets grew faster than the U.S. market because there

ハレー彗星
1986
HALLEY'S COMET
A VIEWER'S GUIDE
WITH
WILLIAM SHATNER

were fewer entertainment alternatives—fewer TV stations, restricted viewing hours, fewer pay TV services and fewer movie theaters.

Domestic Market Share

These manufacturers currently hold the following market shares in the domestic video market according to *Video Week/Home Viewer*, January 6, 1986, Vol. 7, No. 1.

	$ Sales (millions)	**% Share**	**Unit Sales** (millions)
CBS/Fox*	227	13.5	5.5-5.75
Vestron**	175	10.4	4.25-4.5
RCA/Columbia	170	10.1	4.25-5
MGM/UA	151	9	3.75-4
Warner	139	8.3	3.25-3.5
Paramount	139	8.3	5.5-5.75
MCA	118	7	2.75-3
Disney	104	6.2	3.25-3.5
Thorn-EMI-HBO	104	6.2	2.5-2.75
Embassy	60	3.6	1.5
Media	54	3.2	2-2.5
New World	40	2.4	1
Karl-Lorimar	40	2.4	1.25-1.5
IVE***	40	2.4	1.5-1.75
Prism	20	1.2	.5-.75
Western	17	1	2.8
All others	67	4	—

(Source: Video Week, 1985 Television Digest Inc.)
* Includes Key Video and Playhouse
** Includes Lightning Video
*** Includes Family Home Entertainment, USA, Monterey

New Market Outlets

There are also markets developing beyond the traditional video store. (It seems funny to call something *"traditional"* that's only been in existence for a few years!) The other outlets that rent tapes are convenience stores, drugstores and grocery stores. There is a potential universe of 40,000 drugstores and grocery stores, 25,000 mass merchandisers, 10,000 record stores, and 15,000 bookstores. According to Video Software Dealers Association, the current children's programming business is about $100 million. Toy stores are becoming an outlet for children's video programs. There are also specialty outlets such as golf shops, tennis shops, sporting goods stores, spas, exercise and fitness classes, health food stores, and others that will broaden the sales opportunities for specialized videotapes.

These new outlets and new forms for emerging programs indicate great opportunities in the next few years for program producers and distributors alike.

Video Retailer Purchase by Genre

According to a Video Software Dealers Association (VSDA) survey the video retailer spent his dollar on:

	1985 In Stores Carrying Adult Prod.	1985 In Stores NOT Carrying Adult Prod.	1984
Action/Adventure	18.5%	23.1%	25.2%
Science Fiction	7.1	9.3	19.6
Adult	10.0	—	13.0
Children's	10.7	12.6	10.4
Comedy	18.5	21.3	8.8

Drama	14.5	15.2	8.6
Horror	11.1	7.5	8.0
Music Video	4.7	4.6	2.9
How-To	2.1	4.8	2.7
Foreign	1.0	0.9	0.8
Sports	1.8	0.7	—
	100.0%	100.0%	100.0%

While movies are the most desired program form to rent and sell, other non-feature forms are finding a niche in the market.

Summary

These statistics give a sense of where we are now and how the video market may develop. Keep in mind this video snapshot of the industry while developing program ideas. These statistics will undoubtedly change dramatically as the industry is still maturing and any number of changes could disrupt the above projections.

However, these numbers can help. As we learn how videotapes are actually sold, we understand it is clear that the total universe of VCRs tells little about how a specific tape will succeed. The real question is *"who are the videotape renters/buyers, how do you reach them, will they want to buy or rent my tape, and at what price?"* Statistics are fascinating but they should be interpreted with great care.

GETTING STARTED

Getting Started

"Is there really a need for the tape, beyond your own desire to make it?"

Getting Started

Don't even think of beginning to design a program until you have some knowledge of the marketplace. (We'll review it in greater depth in later chapters.) The objective, of course, is to design something that a distributor will want to handle, that a video store will rent, or hopefully, that a consumer will want to buy. Once you've done your homework, the fun begins with how to figure out the best form for your video program so that it will meet the various needs of the distributor, wholesaler, retailer and viewer. First, ask yourself, what do you want to create? What is the subject—gardening, exercise, travel, game, personal finance? How will you treat your subject—didactically, balanced viewpoint, comedic, animation, dramatically? Does the subject have other potential markets besides home video, like pay TV, broadcast TV, foreign theatrical? Are there specific content restrictions, such as censorship, that must be met? Is program length a factor? Will the material translate successfully in another medium (like TV) or be understood in another country? Can a book, album, audiotape or concert be spun-off?

You may only have a vague notion of what you want to do. Sketch out as much as you can about the program—what elements it contains, its length, its intended use, how it will be sold, its price. Write down these key points. You will wish to research them further by talking with producers and distributors. If you hire a writer to focus and embellish your idea, he or she will want to know as much as possible about your proposed idea.

SOURCES OF IDEAS

Pre-Existing Material

If you are a producer looking for ideas for videotape programs, seek out pre-existing video material from movies, new and old TV shows, foreign films, public domain footage. There are numerous possibilities for *"compilations"* designed around footage that already exists. (Of course, this footage cannot be used without compensation. The rights holders will need to be paid for any use of their materials.) Study the market. Is there really a need for the tape you've dreamed up, beyond your own desire to make it?

Celebrity Participation

Once you have a strong idea, get a celebrity to participate. This will give the project a necessary pre-promoted element and increase its attractiveness to the end-user. Regardless of the content, you need a hook. A celebrity may help where a specific subject may not have any inherent appeal by itself. Actors, musicians and politicians often have personal interests, pet causes, hobbies or other talents they may wish to convey through a videotape. If a celebrity is a supporter of a certain worthy cause, you may gain his or her cooperation for little or no fee. If you read popular magazines like *People* or *US* you can learn about celebrities' interests. You may find celebrities and well-known personalities for causes like child abuse, drunk-driving prevention, cancer research, the homeless, world hunger and other topics. Their participation brings added value to your tape. It gives you a handle for marketing the tape—especially if they also agree to help promote it for you.

Debbie Does Las Vegas
Starring
DEBBIE
REYNOLDS
DEBBIE DOES LAS VEGAS Starring DEBBIE REYNOLDS
Produced by JACKIE BARNETT Directed by PAUL SMITH
Staged by ROBERT SIDNEY Musical Creative Consultant RUDI RENDER
Costumes by BOB MACKIE
Released in Association with PAUL BROWNSTEIN PRODUCTIONS, INC.

Recent large-scale examples of celebrity participation were the music videos by *Band Aid* and *U.S.A. For Africa*, which raised money for hunger in Ethiopia, the *Sun City* music video against apartheid in South Africa, and the *Comic Relief* concert where numerous comics raised funds for America's homeless. There are countless examples of smaller projects such as Henry Winkler's participation in Paramount's *Strong Kids, Safe Kids* and Lindsay Wagner in *Touch*, both dealing with child molestation.

Video Stores/Catalogs

The marketplace itself is a source for ideas. Visit your local video store. Study catalogs from videotape distributors. Develop a feel for what exists and what has worked before. See if you can find niches in the market where programming doesn't exist. Look to other forms of media for ideas (newspapers, magazines, TV news, music, books). You may find more projects not to do but somewhere there may be just one . . .

Corporate Sponsors

Sponsors have just begun to explore using video. They look toward enhancing their corporate image, demonstrating products and services and returning a profit. Some sponsors may finance a tape, assist with its promotion, or buy back tapes to give away with high priced products as a premium. For example, Nike, the running shoe manufacturer, may contribute money to a how-to on jogging or to finance a women's marathon as well as provide advertisements when it comes time to sell a tape. Pepsi may sponsor a rock concert or tape that would appeal to a soft-drink audience. Miller Beer might be interested in a tape on a sporting event or personality. The possibilities of matching sponsor and subject are varied.

Red Lobster restaurants sponsored the tape *''Eat To Win''* (Karl Video, 1985) based on the best-selling book. The first release of three *National Geographic* videos was duplicated on TDK tape. TDK took out

VHS
#1
THE PHENOMENAL NATIONWIDE BESTSELLER!
EAT TO WIN
THE SPORTS NUTRITION BIBLE
Red Lobster
$39.95
SUGGESTED RETAIL PRICE
HOSTED BY
DR. ROBERT HAAS
STARRING
JUDY LANDERS
SPECIAL APPEARANCES BY IVAN LENDL
AUDREY LANDERS
KARL HOME VIDEO

consumer ads that touted National Geographic and the quality of its tape. Develop ways that your program could be of use to corporate sponsors and then go talk with them. You may discover they have ideas of their own they wish to finance.

Publishers

I'd venture a guess that every publisher—and not just the megapublisher—has books already in print, or manuscripts in development or ideas for video programs. With all the press about original home video programs, publishers will be the first to revisit their idea lists.

There are hundreds of publishers releasing nearly 40,000 books per year! Undoubtedly there are a few good ideas there! Some will be adaptable to video, others won't. There are plenty of ideas—but don't be seduced by them. Test the market to see if such a tape would actually rent or sell through the outlets currently available. Attend regional publishing fairs or the American Booksellers' Association (ABA) convention to see the new book lines. Or, just browse through your local bookstore or library and ask yourself if anything you see suggests a video program.

Title Invention

Some exploitational film producers invent titles first and hire writers later to create a script! They test market a title and package art to see if there is significant interest before they produce the film. Video producers can do likewise. Gather your collaborators. Disconnect the phone. *"Title jam"* around the desired theme or genre. Create a massive list of potential titles. Take the best titles and have an art director do sketches. Who said you can't design the cover art for the

STEVE MARTIN
LIVE!
In
"Homage To Steve"
And
The Absent Minded Waiter
THE ABSENT-MINDED WAITER A STEVE MARTIN Short
Written by STEVE MARTIN Directed by CARL GOTTLIEB
with BUCK HENRY and TERI GARR
Produced by THE ASPEN FILM SOCIETY
HOMAGE TO STEVE "Concert Segment" Directed by GARY WEIS
Produced by JOE CATES
"Comedians Segment" Written and Directed by STEVE MARTIN
Produced by RANDY COHEN

cassette box before you decide what you're going to put in it? Write copy hooks. This will help refine your ideas for the program itself. The best titles and copy hooks can then be refined and tested with video distributors, wholesalers, retailers, media buyers, librarians and end-users. Produce a winner.

Video Source Book

There are pitfalls. Don't work in a vacuum. Don't let your own interest in a particular subject run away with you. Study what's already out there. Most of the 100 projects that are pitched weekly at Vestron Video have already been done! I can't stress enough—study what's already out there. Save yourself considerable time and money. The *Video Source Book* (published by National Video Clearinghouse) lists 40,000 videotape programs categorized by subject. Check whether your idea has already been produced. If so, isn't that worth knowing? On the other hand, if a similar title exists, that doesn't mean there's no further opportunity. If you find a similar title, screen it. If it was produced 20 years ago, it could need updating.

Keep It Simple

Once you've started to plan, keep your concept simple. Don't mix genres. If you are doing a comedy, do a comedy. If you are doing an exercise tape, do an exercise tape. Mixing genres does not make a better tape. One producer started out to make an exercise tape, got carried away, and threw in some sex and comedy. Then he added music and edited it like a music video. A sports star was the host. Confusing? You bet. There was no way to clearly market it. It wasn't funny enough to be a comedy, not sexy enough to arouse, nor substantial enough for the exercise enthusiast. The tape couldn't provide everything, although it tried. *Remember: Don't mix genres. More isn't better.*

Brainstorm

The time to throw in all your good ideas is in the development stage. You can try anything. It won't cost you anything. When you're in production you should already know what you want to accomplish. But before then, let your imagination run wild.

Everything you see, everyone you talk to, every place you go, everything you visualize, everything you hear will give you ideas. If you allow yourself to think freely and luxuriously, you can always impose the necessary market limitations later.

Once you've brainstormed hundreds of ideas, begin giving yourself some focus. Sprinkle in some guidelines that reflect the limitations in the marketplace. Not every idea makes sense in home video. Your conscious mind knows this, your unconscious mind doesn't really care. Once you've established these guidelines *("I want to make an hour-long comedy with women only as a rental video")* then set your unconscious mind loose for concepts, casting, titles, and packaging.

Sometimes you may struggle coming up with an idea for a title. By consciously working on it you may get nowhere. Give your unconscious mind an assignment (to come up with a title). Then go on to think about something else entirely. At the same time you propose the problem, also ask your unconscious mind to deliver the goods—as when you start your car in the morning or when you open the door to your office. This works for me more often than not and frees my conscious mind for other thinking. I can relax knowing that sooner or later I'll get the idea I couldn't find any other way.

The book, *A Whack on the Side of the Head: How to Unlock Your Mind for Innovation,* by Roger von Oech, is loaded with other approaches to the creative process, which you can apply to program development. The best place to begin is at the beginning—with a strong idea.

OPPORTUNITIES FOR INDEPENDENTS

Opportunities for Independents

"It takes about a year for a consumer to see all their favorite movies...then what?"

Opportunities for Independents

The studios produce feature films that find their way into the video store four to six months after theatrical release. Major and minor independent producers also contribute a healthy share of low-budgeted genre pictures: action, adventure, sexploitation, westerns, and horror. It takes a consumer about a year to go through his or her 50 must-see movies before he or she will begin to seek out other forms of programming. In addition, Hollywood has already released nearly 75% of all old films stored in its vaults. There's not much more. This is good news for independent producers with non-feature program ideas.

Feature producers have already identified film genres that can be successful in the theatrical market. What follows is a brief overview of non-feature original program genres that have already proved to be successful. There are also many emerging genres that will be explored in depth in later chapters. Producers may first however wish to examine these pre-set genres because they work—they can be sold and marketed successfully.

OVERVIEW OF GENRES

Comedy

Comedy is a proven genre in both feature films and home video. Comedy can be conceived as episodic, compilation (Groove Tube style), straight stand-up, parody, or concept. In the comedy area, stand-up performances by Richard Pryor (sold over 20,000 units) and Father Guido Sarducci have done well. Joe Piscopo, Bill Cosby, Billy Crystal, George Carlin, Gallagher, Weird Al, and old clips of Three Stooges have all sold 5,000-10,000 units—which, for an original program, is quite good. Retail prices range from $29 to $59.

Compilations

Compilations of previously existing material include *That Was Rock* (Media Home Entertainment), *Candid Candid Camera* with Allen Funt (Vestron), *Hollywood Outtakes* (RCA/Columbia), *Academy Award Winners: Animated Short Films* (Vestron), *The Compleat Beatles* (MGM/UA), *Best of 60 Minutes* (CBS/Fox), *Amazing Masters of the Martial Arts* (Vestron). These and others have sold well, pointing to compilations as a potential new genre for home video programming.

Erotic

Erotic (non X-rated) programs that have seen success in home video are the *Playboy Video* Series (CBS/Fox, now on Karl/Lorimar), *The Girls of Rock and Roll* (CBS/Fox), *Penthouse Video* (Vestron), *Party Games for Adults Only* (MCA) and *Girls Nite Out* (Thorn/EMI).

Biographies/Personalities

Biographies of well-known personalities have demonstrated some success. Examples are *The Jane Mansfield Story* (USA Video), *The*

Jesse Owens Story (Paramount), *The Legend of Valentino* (Prism), *This Is Elvis* (Warner Home Video), and *Rita Hayworth: The Love Goddess* (USA). Current personalities like Vestron's *The Beach Boys: An American Band, The Prince and Princess of Wales: Talking Personally* and RCA/Columbia's *Iaccoca* are also popular.

Exercise

The big successes have come in the exercise genre with such megahits as the Jane Fonda series (*Workout, Challenge, Pregnancy, Prime Time*—Karl/Lorimar Video). Successful tapes also include *Raquel: Total Beauty and Fitness* (Thorn/EMI), *Do It Debbie's Way* (Video Associates), *The Armed Forces Workout* (Vestron), *The 20-Minute Workout* (Vestron), *Body by Jake* (MCA), *Everyday with Richard Simmons* (Karl), *Aerobic Dancing* (MCA), *Mary Lou Retton* (Karl/Lorimar) and *Mousercise* (Disney). But that doesn't mean that all exercise tapes do well. There have been over 180 produced to date and only a handful have made money.

Documentaries

Only a few documentaries have been released and these have achieved rather small sales but this is slowly changing. Those with exploitable subject matter or highly promotable titles perform best. Remember, they must compete with movies. Examples are: *The Great Movie Stunts: Making of the Raiders of the Lost Ark* (Paramount), *Kennedys Don't Cry* (MPI), *Witchcraft Through the Ages* (Embassy), *The World at War* (Volumes 1-26) (Thorn/EMI), *Chicken Ranch* (Vestron), *Hooker* (Vestron), *Murder: No Apparent Motive* (Vestron), *From Mao to Mozart* (Karl).

National Geographic Video, a series from Vestron that includes *Land of the Tiger, The Sharks*, and *Iceland River Breakthrough* are among the best-selling documentaries yet released. In this case you have a highly recognizable quality name that transcends the subject matter and is sold at a collectible price of $29.

How-To

How-tos or instructional tapes have been made in just about every conceivable category. Just when you think you've seen the last of them, a whole new series springs up. There are how-tos on language, dance, sports, fishing, childbirth, parenting, diet, sex, fun learning, health, music, travel, garden, home repair, car repair, cooking, education, smoking, seduction, swimming, crime prevention and so on ad infinitum. Both production values and retail prices have been low. Producers are hopeful that this genre will someday be as popular as are their counterparts on bookstore shelves. Perhaps consumers will buy low-priced instructional programming, but so far sales have been extremely small. Most video retailers have been soft on this form of programming so distributors have resorted to direct response promotion through direct mail and magazine space advertising.

When a how-to subject is combined with a celebrity or recognized authority, then bookstores and other specialty stores are more likely to consider carrying the title. Right now the distribution channels are somewhat imperfect and are incapable of delivering any spectacular numbers. Paramount's *Strong Kids, Safe Kids* sold well (30,000 units). However, given that Paramount spent over $100,000 on the promotional campaign, it should have done better. The distributor may not have broken even, given these expenses and a $250,000 budget.

Children

Children's programming is undoubtedly the most promising of the non-feature program genres. Unlike other forms of programming, children's tapes are automatically *"repeatable."* A child will enthusiastically watch a favorite program 30 to 50 times! Parents therefore find more value in buying the tape than in continuously renting it. The most successful children's fare has been animations of recognizable licensed characters drawn from broadcast television and repackaged. These programs and the characters contained within have the greatest visibility with children. The most popular titles are from Disney, Sesame Street, and from well-known characters such as *Rainbow Bright* and *My Little Pony* (Vestron), *The Care Bears* (Vestron and Family Home Entertainment), *Transformers* (Family Home Entertainment), and so on. Besides programs based on recognizable characters, the popular classics have performed well. CBS/Fox has proved this by going *''gold''* with sales of 20,000 units with titles like *Snow White and the Seven Dwarfs, Sleeping Beauty, Rapunzel, Beauty and the Beast, Goldilocks and the Three Bears, Tale of the Frog Prince,* and *Jack and the Beanstalk.* Western Publishing's *Golden Book Videos*, like *Best Loved Book Favorites, Richard Scarry, Best Loved Golden Books, He-Man and the Masters of the Universe,* priced at $9.95, have become some of the best-selling children's titles ever by distributing through toy stores, mass merchants, and video stores.

Music

Music video, to date, has been disappointing. Hopes were high when *Making Michael Jackson's Thriller* (Vestron) sold a million units worldwide. Other successes have been few and far between although there have been many attempts. The reason for this is more obvious when you think about it. At present the majority of people who buy records are between the ages of 12 and 18. They do not have video machines. At least not yet. Parents, between the ages of 25 and 45, are the ones with the machines. So there is a mismatch. Music videos are being offered to a market that doesn't yet have the hardware to play them. Until there are video players in the kid's room, numbers will be small, while program production costs remain high. But as the price of VCRs drops, and second machines come into the home, music video will pick up.

Another reason for the lack of appeal of music video is that a tremendous amount of music video is available free on MTV and the other cable and broadcast networks. Why pay for it? And, in most cases, by the time the video is released, the song is old news. The simultaneous release of the album and video has not, until recently, been well sequenced. Peter Townsend's *White City* album and long form video (Vestron) were promoted and released simultaneously, thus cross-promoting and maximizing the title's success.

Sources for Original Programs

The preceding are just some of the more successful pre-set genres. Since these genres have been successful it benefits a producer to focus along these pre-developed lines.

Where does a producer look for original program ideas? The sources for original programming are as varied as the programs themselves, and range from off-network television fare to children's licensed characters, compilation of pre-existing film and video tape footage, book titles, music acts, magazine articles, instructional properties, etc. All are areas that producers can explore.

The next chapter will break down these and other genres so that a producer may grasp what has been successful and why. What are the elements in each genre that make a successful original program? The models for original programming are constantly changing. A single hit (such as *Jane Fonda's Workout*) can serve as the launching pad for hundreds of other exercise programs. It is important for producers to see where we've been so they will know where they are going.

GENRES OF ORIGINAL PROGRAMMING

Genres of Original Programming

''If the idea is really hot, distributors will be tripping all over themselves to take you to lunch.''

Genres of Original Programming

Here begins an adventuresome journey through a myriad of original programming forms and genres. Traditionally, most of these programs are rented by the video specialty store, but in 1985 the sale market started to take hold as a result of expanded distribution to other outlets (mass merchants, toy stores, bookstores) and because of lower pricing. Even the video stores, which are primarily in the rental business, increased their income through sales. A recent Video Marketing survey found that rentals account for 79% and sales for 21% of dollar volume at the retail level. This ratio is expected to increase. This is good news for original program producers because consumers may someday buy tapes the same way they now buy hardcover books and record albums.

In 1985 the average rental price was $6.90 and the average sales price was $42.66. Prices are still dropping. By the time you read this they will be even lower. When prices fall below $29 there will be an even greater incentive to buy. The purchase may be impulsive as it is in the book trade. Original programs, if they can be made to be collectible or repeatable or possess some added value, are prime candidates for lower pricing and ownership.

In 1984 original programming (non-features) accounted for approximately 10% (or $90 million) of the $900 million home video business. Some project it to generate 25% of gross revenues by 1990. There is every indication that original program video publishing will be a very healthy and substantial business in the future. The time to get aboard is now.

Feature Film Environment

Producers would benefit by visiting their local video stores when they are designing original programs. Spend a few hours seeing how customers respond to packaging, how and when titles are selected, and how cassettes are displayed on the shelf. You'll see that the retail store is a feature film environment. Retailers buy movies for consumers to rent. It's already a way of life. Since it is a feature film environment, the more an original program looks and feels like a movie, the more readily acceptable it will be by both the retailer (who is the first buyer of the program) and the consumer (who is the renter and possible purchaser). This is, of course, not always the case, but it is a good place to start when analyzing the market and determining how to design your programs.

This is not to say that original programs will sell as many units as the average feature film. Because home video is primarily a movie-driven business, it is not unusual for producers to overestimate the potential sales of programs. (They think original programs will sell as well as movies—they don't.) Subsequently, they spend too much money producing their shows because they expect their original programs to sell like a feature. It just won't happen. Without a multimillion dollar ad campaign (such as movies have) the retailer will never have heard of an original program and probably won't be very interested. Pre-promotion is everything. So, unless it is produced well, but cheaply, and highly promoted, it is unlikely that an original program will recoup its production cost from the home video alone. An average movie may sell 40,000 units or more, but an average original program in 1985 may only sell 3,000, 5,000, 10,000 or 20,000 units. And at less than movie retail prices.

Unless your program is suitable for sale to bookstores or mass merchandisers (and many aren't), you only have a customer base of 20,000—the mom-and-pop video stores. If you sell just one cassette per store, you've got a hit. It sounds easy, but it isn't. Most stores are offered 500 a month by wholesalers. They may buy only 10, 20 or 30 different titles. Why will yours be one of them? Just because you think every drugstore, convenience store, toy store and mass outlet should carry your tape, it doesn't mean they will. Of the 500 titles released each month, very few are sold in non-traditional video outlets. If you design your program so that it has the potential of being sold into other markets, you enhance your recoupment potential.

What follows is a more in-depth exploration of original program genres, forms that currently exist and those forms that are emerging. Within each genre there may be sub-genres or sub-forms such as in the comedy genre.

Comedy

Comedy is a popular genre in feature films and in original programs. Comedy is successful on network and pay television. There are a variety of forms in comedy for original programs. Most shows vary in length between 60 and 80 minutes.

There is the straight stand-up show, which is little more than a comedian's performance in front of a microphone. This requires minimal production expense beyond talent fees. Examples of this are the performance tapes of Richard Pryor, Eddie Murphy, George Carlin and Gallagher (who uses props in his act). *Father Guido Sarducci Goes to College* (Vestron) is essentially a stand-up show but contains many minutes of concept wrap-arounds with Sarducci in the Vatican, his arrival on campus, his romp with coeds, his stand-up routine with slide

Father Guido Sarducci
GOES TO COLLEGE
FROM SATURDAY NIGHT LIVE
FATHER GUIDO SARDUCCI
IN HIS FIRST HOME
VIDEO PERFORMANCE!
Starring FATHER GUIDO SARDUCCI
With Special Guest Stars
FATHER BILLY VERA & THE BEATERS
Produced & Directed By STEVE BINDER
Written by DON NOVELLO

show (the bulk of the show), a question and answer session with students, and a closing musical number. Although it was based around a stand-up performance, writer Don Novello (Sarducci) and director Steve Binder found ways to increase the value of the video to be something more than stand-up.

The frustrating thing for a developer of comedy is that there are many talented young, up-and-coming comedians with polished acts that are difficult to market. They are unknowns, and unless you have an overwhelmingly hot concept, the tapes will simply not be bought. Appearing on Carson or Letterman is not enough. This points to the importance of pre-exposure and pre-promotion.

There are exceptions. Whoopie Goldberg's one-woman show on Broadway was a knockout last year but who, then, had heard of her? I saw her when people asked *''What's a Whoopie Goldberg?''* However, given Whoopie's enormous talent it was obvious that it would only be a matter of time before she would hit.

So, we *''stretched''* for the program and paid more for the show than it was worth at the time. It paid off. A few months later it was announced that she'd play the lead in Spielberg's new film, *The Color Purple*. Later she received an Academy Award nomination for Best Actress. Vestron took orders on the tape at Academy Awards time when news about Whoopi was everywhere. Her album received a Grammy for best comedy album and a special sticker was printed about the award and applied to the cassette jacket. The tape was very successful. Pre-promotion and timing was perfect.

Producers with vision can utilize this strategy in producing shows—but few distributors will take the chance with an unknown. A producer must be careful in becoming a *''believer''* when selecting unknown comics; just because they are funny doesn't mean success is right around the corner.

The comedy vignette is another form that comedy can take. The *Joe*

The acclaimed
Golden Globe Award-winner
of Steven Spielberg's
"THE COLOR PURPLE"!
Whoopi Goldberg
Executive Producer SANDY GALLIN
Produced by WHOOP, Inc. in association with BROADWAY VIDEO and D.I.R. Broadcasting
Directed by THOMAS SCHLAMME
All material written and performed by WHOOPI GOLDBERG
Production supervised by MIKE NICHOLS
Based on an original HBO presentation

Bette Midler
ART OR BUST
EXPANDED FEATURE-LENGTH VERSION! CONTAINS OVER 20 MINUTES OF ADDITIONAL PERFORMANCES!
"...THE DIVINE MISS M. AT HER BEST...CLASS AND SASS."
—The Hollywood Reporter
"...AN ASTONISHING PERFORMER."
—The New York Times
"A DELIGHT."
—People Magazine
In her own outrageous way, Bette Midler takes on the world of art—and comes out as a shining superstar—in this uniquely funny, naughty, bawdy, raunchy, unpredictable and stunningly visual video concert.
ART OR BUST is the theme, and you'll see Bette mastering the masters, becoming an animated modern madonna and basically singing her (considerable) heart out. The impact of her songs is made all the more exciting by extraordinary special effects and costumes. And finally, when she and her backup singers, the Harlettes, don mermaid costumes and hop in motorized wheelchairs for a wild rendition of "We Are Family," you can't help but get caught up in Bette's incandescent energy, dazzling choreography and stupendous voice.
This special home video version also contains new material not seen on the original ART OR BUST concert: Bette's final performance at the Continental Baths, and the infamous telethon where Bette "drops her dress for Israel," plus other performances. For Bette Midler fans and musical spectacle lovers everywhere, make it "Bette"—or BUST!
VESTRON VIDEO
© 1984 Vestron Video
P.O. Box 4000
Stamford, CT 06907
VHS: VA3080; Beta: VB3080; 82 Minutes; 1984.
Beta
VHS
Printed in U.S.A.

Piscopo Video (Vestron) is far more than a straight stand-up. It is actually a compilation of highly produced sketches with continuity sequences holding it together. In the continuity, Joe is himself; in the skits he plays characters. The various three- to eight-minute skits have elaborate sets, costumes, and makeup, lots of special effects, and several music videos.

The budget was well over $500,000. Had HBO and Vestron not combined forces, it would have been impossible to produce this hour-long video. The producer worked with both entities so that each received the show he needed. Both Vestron and HBO had input into the script. Bette Midler prepared two versions of her show, *Art or Bust:* an hour for HBO, and a 75-minute show for Vestron. Whoopie did the same (the language could be more outrageous in the 75-minute home video version). For large budget comedies, producers should seek several partners for financing.

TV comedy compilations, both old and new, can be assembled by producers. This can be as simple as selecting the best takes or scenes from a television show, and adding wrap-arounds or interstitial material as connective tissue. Examples would be: *The Best of John Belushi* (Warner Home Video), *Jackie Gleason's The Honeymooners* (Maljack), or *The Best of Candid Camera* (Vestron).

There are also off-network specials such as the *Dean Martin Celebrity Roast*. There are re-dubbed foreign features, such as Woody Allen's *What's Up Tiger Lily?*

Comedy videos can also be episodic. One or more comics can play continuing characters and move from episodic vignette to vignette. This allows a producer to use the traditional narrative structure (three acts) with a minimum of expense paid to continuing characters.

Best-selling comedy books serve as excellent source materials. Vestron bought the rights to *Truly Tasteless Jokes* and produced a comedy video program of blue comics performing truly tasteless material. MCA

OFF THE WALL
Today's hottest young comics are the perfect entertainment for your customer's party!
A great party tape of off-the-wall comedy comes to home video with NEW WAVE COMEDY! Watch some of today's most brilliant up-and-coming young comedians including ERIC BOGOSIAN, JOHN KASSIR (TV's "Star Search" comedy winner), STEVE SWEENEY ("Back To School" with Rodney Dangerfield), MARGARET SMITH ("The Blues Brothers") and PATTY ROSBOROUGH ("The World According To Garp") as they show off their best stand-up comedy!
NATIONAL RELEASE DATE: JULY 30, 1986
VHS: VA3128; Beta: VB3128; 60 Minutes.
© 1986 Vestron Video
1011 High Ridge Road
P.O. Box 4000
Stamford, CT 06907
VESTRON VIDEO™
Creative Marketing Company of the Year (as voted by the readers of VIDEO INSIDER)
NEW WAVE COMEDY
"A VIDEOTAPE BY MITCHELL KRIEGMAN"

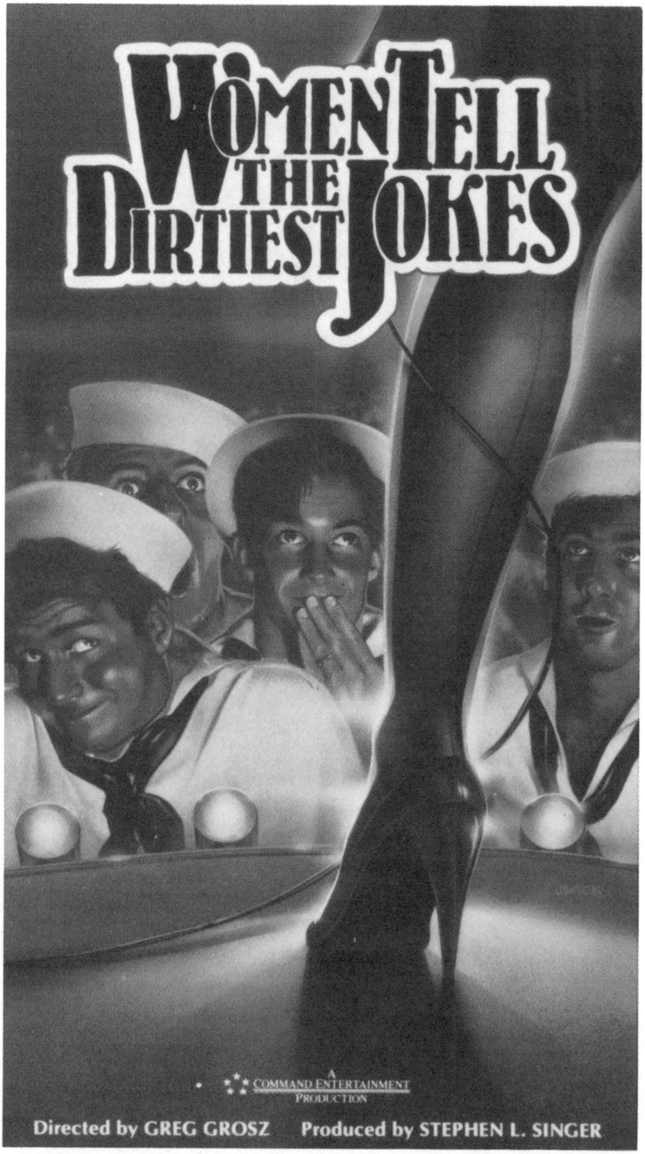
WOMEN TELL THE DIRTIEST JOKES
A COMMAND ENTERTAINMENT PRODUCTION
Directed by GREG GROSZ
Produced by STEPHEN L. SINGER

followed with a *"me-too"* show based on the book: *Gross Jokes*. In both cases, the books pre-promoted the video program and gave the tapes visibility. It was not necessary to employ name talent.

Producers can also come up with high concept titles that bring enough heat to the program to interest the video trade. Vestron fully financed the high concept comedy shows *New Wave Comedy* and *Women Tell the Dirtiest Jokes*. Both utilized young comics (*Star Search* winner John Kassir, Mark Weiner, Eric Bogosian, and *Sanford and Son's* La Wanda Page) with some possibility of breaking through. Moreover, production costs are considerably lower with lesser-known talent and thus fewer cassettes have to sell to be profitable.

Comedy dramas that have been made for pay television may also have a life in home video. The HBO comedies *Best Legs in the Eighth Grade* (Vestron) and *First and Ten* (Vestron) are examples. Each has some recognizable names in the cast.

Some Broadway and off-Broadway shows are home video possibilities if the concept is hot, the talent recognizable, and if other financing partners (pay TV, foreign TV) can be brought to the table.

Cartoon and humor books may also serve as source material from which animations can be created. Characters like Garfield (the cat) offer comedy possibilities. Adult cartoons could also work in home video. A combination of animation and live action might also work, but be careful about combining genres and creating something that won't be marketable.

Comedy compilations of shorts also offer possibilities. *Comedy Videos* (Vestron) is a compilation of three- to four-minute comedic music videos by well-known stars such as Mel Brooks, John Belushi, Dan Ackroyd, John Candy, Bob and Ray, Gary Trudeau and others. Their names and pictures are featured on the cassette package. The most difficult part of putting this kind of show together is clearing the music and picture rights. Producers who lack patience and experience should

RICHARD PRYOR
Live and Smokin'
The funniest comedian of
our time in his very first
complete, uncensored
live concert performance.
Includes
"The Wino
and
The Junkie"
A Michael Blum Production

avoid compilations. Rights must be cleared from all the rights holders in the original material. It is expensive and time consuming to negotiate these rights.

What you get by compiling short programs under one umbrella is the ability to mix promotable names with lesser-known names. The concept for the compilation should also be promotable.

Elements that bring value to a comedy program are: 1) well-known comics, 2) a high concept title, 3) previous exposure (such as a best-selling book, well-known event, etc.), and 4) any additional promotable element you can dream up. Sometimes you can get stars to appear in cameos. Costs are held down and you can obtain a promotable element you may not otherwise have.

In 1985, programs with stars other than Richard Pryor, Robin Williams, Billy Crystal, Gallagher and a few others probably sold between 3,000 and 7,000 units. There are too many programs in the marketplace. However, today's sales figures shouldn't deter producers from going after tomorrow's hit. The marketplace changes every few months. As the sell-through market develops and retail prices fall, there will be a greater opportunity to sell more tapes.

Prices for comedy range from $29.95 for the *Three Stooges* (RCA/ Columbia) to $39.95, for *Comedy Tonight* (K-Tel) to $59.95 for *Richard Pryor: Live and Smokin'* (Vestron). Examples of unit sales (when the tape was first shipped—called *''out of the box''*) are approximately 7,000 to 8,000 units for *Gallagher* (Paramount), 3,000 for *David Steinberg*, 650 for *Franken and Davis at Stockton* (Pacific Arts), 3,500 for *George Burns in Concert* (USA) and 1,700 for *The Lily Tomlin Special* (Karl). *Richard Pryor: Live and Smoking* (Vestron) sold more than 20,000 units and was certified *''gold.''* Some figures appear unusually low. The tapes may not have received the necessary promotion by the distributor.

When a tape sells at $29.95 retail, the wholesale price is about $20. The

15% royalty (from the wholesale price) is $3 per unit. If a tape sells 10,000 units, the producer's royalties are $30,000. Consequently the producer should either find another market (like pay TV) to cover production costs.

It's a different story when the same tape is priced high. When a tape sells for $59.95, then the wholesale price is about $38. The 15% royalty is $5.70. If the tape sells 10,000 units then the royalty is $57,000, nearly double the income. The retail price is obviously an important factor. Producers should have an idea how their tape will be priced when striking a distribution deal.

If a 1985 program was made for pay TV and home video, a producer could expect three-fourths or five-sixths of the budget to come from pay TV and the balance from home video, assuming, of course, it was of value to both markets. The trick is to find a project that is promotable, has stars and is desirable to both pay TV and home video. There are no hard rules. If a program is desirable enough, both partners may put up more dollars than the production cost, assuring the producer a profit on day one!

Producers will find that different home video distributors and different pay TV networks will place different values on the same program. Some will reject what others find to be valuable. This happens every day. I have acquired programs that no other distributor wanted, found a unique way to promote it and made money. At the same time, I've passed on projects that later received large advances from other home video companies.

In comedy, or in any other program genre, it's really up to the producer to put together the best elements he can, design a highly promotable package, and offer it to a distributor. If the producer has done his or her homework, then the program should be appealing. Homework means studying the programs already in release, designing and producing a program that will have appeal to the wholesaler, the retailer and the consumer. It's fun, it's creative, and there are still many exciting and profitable programs to be made.

Documentaries

Documentaries have been a difficult form for television and home video. For example, whenever surveys are done for PBS or pay television, and people are asked if they want to see more documentaries, they inevitably answer *"yes."* But they lie. People do so because they want to appear intelligent. When documentaries are actually broadcast, those that say *"yes"* are inevitably watching the *A-Team*. The same is true for those home video polls. People say they wish they could rent them but not really. (There are some notable exceptions, which we'll get to in a moment.) Since tapes are being sold in a movie environment in the video retail store, then the documentary should have a movie-ish feel to it. Can your documentary subject be marketed as a family or action adventure? Does it have a tantalizing, easily promotable title? How can it be positioned to appeal more to the movie trade? If your documentary can be dressed like a movie, it will stand a better chance competing against the real movies. My own television special documentary *Dolphin* was retitled *Dolphin Adventures* (Vestron) to give it a better position in the marketplace. It received a very limited theatrical release and review quotes will be used in the campaign.

My sense is that there are two kinds of documentaries that could find a growing market in the next few years: first, the highly exploitable documentary titles (because of their content), and second, documentaries suited for family viewing, such as animal shows or wildlife adventures.

The exploitable documentaries may have played on PBS, HBO or network television and had *"hot"* themes, such as David Bell Associates' *Hooker* and *Losin' It: Sex and the American Teenager* (both

Hooker
EXECUTIVE PRODUCER DAVE BELL
PRODUCER ANN HASSETT
DIRECTOR ROBERT NIEMACK
EDITOR KEVA ROSENFELD
A DAVE BELL ASSOCIATES PRODUCTION
BASED ON AN ORIGINAL HBO PRESENTATION

The
POLICE
TAPES
VIDEO VERITÉ PRESENTS
THE POLICE TAPES
Produced, Directed and Edited by
ALAN RAYMOND and
SUSAN RAYMOND

Vestron). In some instances broadcast television may have restricted the inclusion of certain sequences or subject matter. Home video has no such restrictions, so the programs could be expanded or re-edited. This was the case with the Bell documentaries just mentioned. Another example is Wendy Apple's *Fallen Angels,* a hard-hitting documentary about the actresses, agents, and producers in the porn business. The themes of these curiosity-provoking documentaries fall outside anything you could see on broadcast television, making them perfect for home video. They contain promotable elements that ensure some interest from the home video trade and the consumer.

High-profile, readily recognizable documentaries for families, like Jacques Cousteau's programs or those produced by *National Geographic*, are perfect for home video. They are well known to consumers and trade alike.

While public knowledge may not exist for its specific shows, National Geographic is a respected and prestigious name we've all grown up with. In 1986 I concluded an agreement with National Geographic to release an entire home video line through Vestron. A year earlier this would not have made sense because the distribution outlets were too few. Today, video retailers, mass merchandisers, book and toy stores have all taken on National Geographic videos and made them top-sellers. The initial releases include the television specials that have been all-time PBS top-rated shows (nine of the top 10). Shows like *Land of The Tiger, The Sharks, The Great Whales* and *Koko: The Gorilla* are all memorable and timeless. Priced at $29.95 retail they are collectible. Parents enjoy them, recognize their quality, and purchase them for their children in the same way they buy encyclopedias. The packaging mirrors the magazine with its familiar yellow border.

Furthermore, have you ever tried to throw out a National Geographic magazine? It's impossible. (The 11th commandment is *"Thou Shalt Never Harm a National Geographic magazine."*) Hopefully, the desire to collect the tapes will be as strong as the desire to collect the

NEW RELEASE
BUILD THE EXCITEMENT!
Build On The Success. Build The Sales. Build Your
National Geographic Video Library—For Even Greater Profits
With The Most Prestigious Name In Family Programming.
NATIONAL GEOGRAPHIC VIDEO
THE INCREDIBLE HUMAN MACHINE
YUKON PASSAGE
NATIONAL GEOGRAPHIC VIDEO

NATIONAL
GEOGRAPHIC
VIDEO
THE SHARKS
Get closer than ever
before to nature's most
fearsome predator.

magazine. The tapes are also being sold by direct mail and through National Geographic magazine ads. The combination of elements—low price, recognizable name, quality, promotable subjects, and multiple markets—make this line of programming ideal for home video distribution—a very unusual combination of elements for documentaries.

There are also compilation-based programs that could be considered documentaries. *The Beach Boys: An American Band* (Vestron), *The Compleat Beatles* (MGM/UA), and *The Doors* (MCA) are examples. Some documentary filmmakers believe that *Making Michael Jackson's Thriller* was successful because it was a documentary. Give me a break! The success of the cassettes mentioned above came about because the films were on world-renowned performers, not because they are documentaries.

Some examples of documentary programs already released are *Battle of Britain* (Victory), *Blue Water White Death* (CBS/Fox), *Children of Theater Street* (Kultur), *The Cousteau Odyssey: The Nile* (Warner), *The Clowns* (Media), *From Mao to Mozart* (Karl), *First Man into Space* (Monterey), *Great Figures in History: JFK* (CBS/Fox), and *The Making of Superman I and II* (USA). Few have sold more than 1,000 to 2,000 units.

As the videotape machine base increases, documentary programming will find a greater niche in the video marketplace. Unfortunately, social and political documentaries do not have a wide enough audience to make current traditional marketing feasible. (A producer with a mailing list to an interested, qualified audience may find limited success with a specialty documentary title—but this is both expensive and difficult to predict.) With the exception of direct marketing, home video is a product for mass market sale of entertainment-based programs.

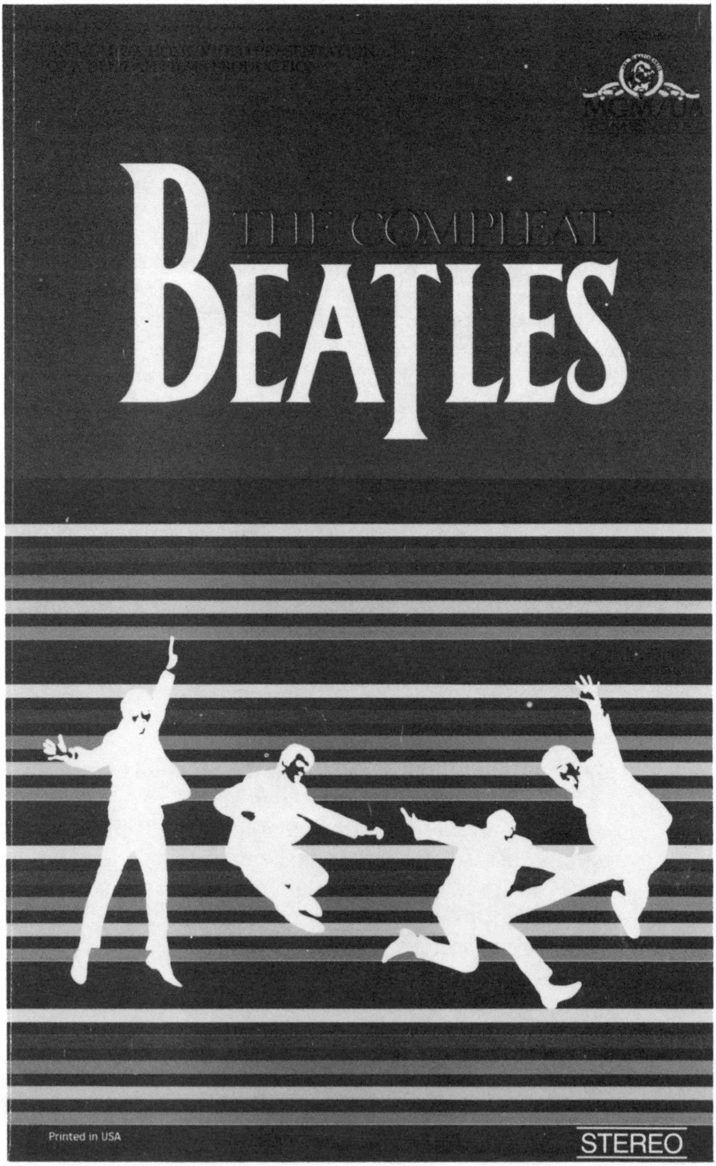
THE COMPLEAT
BEATLES
Printed in USA
STEREO

War

War tapes appeal to history buffs, veterans and some movie buffs—generally an older audience with a VCR and a *"collect them"* attitude, making these tapes perfect for *"sell-through"* marketing.

For some distributors the documentary war series offers an opportunity to establish a *"continuity club."* Once initial sales are made and captured in a mailing list database, consumers can be sold additional tapes in the series. A distributor can profit by the consumers' desire to collect and establish *"negative option"* video clubs where consumers receive tapes automatically and are billed until they choose to stop.

The World at War series (26 volumes) (Thorn/EMI) has sold in excess of 125,000 units, and averages 4,500 units each. *Victory at Sea* (Embassy) and *Battle for the Falklands* have also done remarkably well. The four-volume *45/85: America and the World Since WWII* (Vestron) is a set of one-hour tapes priced at $29.95 each or $99.95 for the set. Maljack distributes Granada Televisions' *From D-Day to Victory in Europe* at $39.95. A Vietnam series should also find an audience.

The following list includes some of the war series videotapes:

Title	**Number**	**Distributor**
Crusade in the Pacific	26	Embassy
Air War Collection	10	
Nostalgia World War II	7	Video Yesteryear
Victory at Sea	26	Embassy
Vietnam: The 10,000 Day War	13	Embassy
Why We Fight	7	MPI
World at War	26	Thorn/EMI
World War II	15	CBS/Fox
45/85: America and The World Since WWII	4	Vestron

THORN EMI VIDEO

VOL. 20 GENOCIDE

The definitive story of World War II, narrated by Sir Laurence Olivier

The footage in these series are in public domain so the shows can be produced cheaply. Many are also from syndicated television so home video revenue is really gravy. Most tapes sell better through direct marketing than through the traditional video retail store.

Erotic

Erotic is a very difficult and tricky genre to define and market. It is differentiated from X-rated programs because it is not X-rated. It is either R-rated or unrated, and not hard-core. But that's hardly a definition.

The difficulty in marketing an erotic program is just that—it doesn't categorize easily. If the retailer puts an erotic program on the X-shelf then the video consumer looking for X-rated material will be disappointed. If it lands on any other shelf, the minister's wife is likely to complain and the video merchant will feel the backlash. Other than the Chippendale tapes and a few others, erotic tapes are mostly male-oriented. However, since X-rated films became available on home video, men, women and yuppies who otherwise would never have ventured to a sleazy porn theater are now renting X-rated tapes. Curiously enough, a recent survey found that more women than men rent X-rated programs. This trend would indicate that producers who made erotic programs for women and couples may find success. In fact, the adaptation of romance novels into home video programs may be the beginning of this trend.

The most highly visible tapes have been those with the *Playboy* or *Penthouse* name. The Playboy tapes are magazine formats (like PM Magazine) with segments—similar to the publication with Playmate interviews and pictorials, short erotic films, and comedy vignettes. The production values are very high due to slick photography, music, costuming and special effects. There are some seven or more volumes

PENTHOUSE
VIDEO
Love Stories

in distribution from CBS/Fox. The first few tapes sold more than 25,000 units but subsequent volumes fell off dramatically because retailers felt they didn't need more than a few Playboy tapes. Playboy later made a distribution deal with Karl/Lorimar who cleverly reformulated the program into a 20-minute cassette with the current Playmate. The tapes are released simultaneously with the magazine and priced at $9.95. After a bumpy start the video magazine found its way to newsstands in selected cities in an innovative marketing push. Others will be sure to follow once this channel proves successful.

Penthouse Video, Volume I and II, (Vestron), features a half-dozen Penthouse pets in fantasy vignettes. The early Playboy and Penthouse tapes are priced at $59. There have also been erotic music video compilations such as *Red Hot Rock* (Vestron) and *The Girls of Rock and Roll* (Playboy). Both were costly productions.

In the erotic genre there are also how-to tapes such as *Playgirl's Sexual Secrets* (which capitalizes on the recognizable magazine) and *Love Skills* (MCA). These tapes have instructional content and are quasi-erotic in form.

Comedy can also offer some possibilities for erotic programming. *Candid Candid Camera*, Volumes I-IV (Vestron) are tapes by Allen Funt with gags along the line of "*What do you say to a naked lady?*" This tape shows unsuspecting people in compromising situations. These rather innocuous programs really aren't erotic but—in the voyeuristic style of *Candid Camera*—they offer enough nudity and comedy to sell well in the U.S. and abroad. Comedy in erotic programming can be just the ticket to taking the edge off sexually oriented programming and differentiating it from the X-product.

The documentaries, *Fallen Angel* (Vestron) about relationships in the porn business, and *Chicken Ranch* (Vestron) about a legal brothel in Nevada may be erotic to some.

Art programs can also be erotic. *Nudes in Limbo* (MCA) was the first

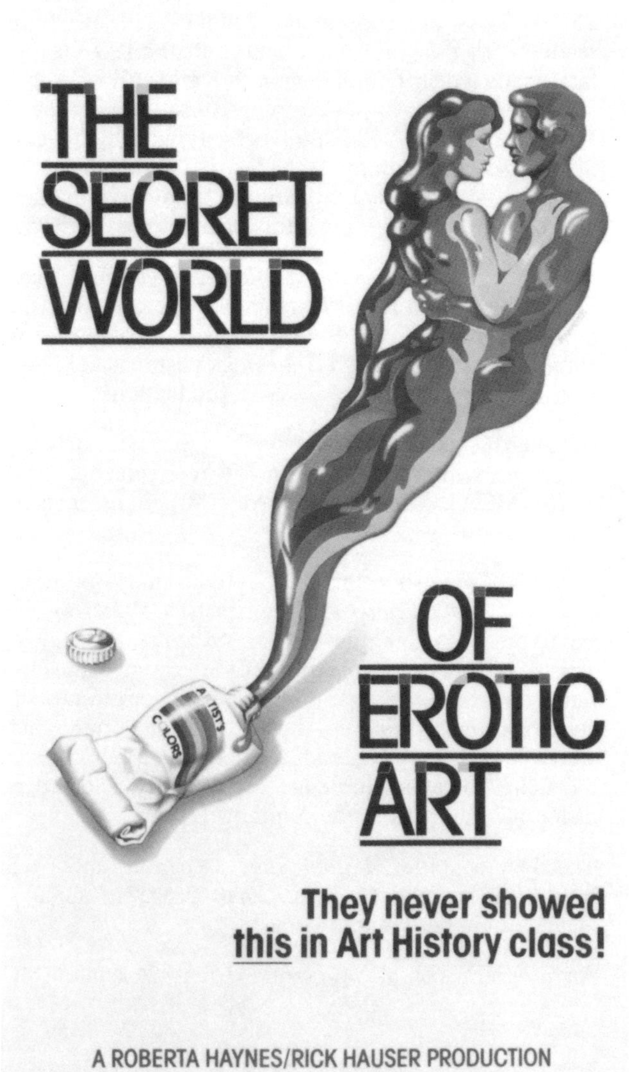
THE SECRET WORLD
OF EROTIC ART
ARTIST'S COLORS
They never showed this in Art History class!
A ROBERTA HAYNES/RICK HAUSER PRODUCTION

soft-core tape by a major studio. *The Secret World of Erotic Art* (Vestron)—the copy read *"they never showed you this in art class"*—is a coffee-table video featuring erotic art by the great master painters. The difficulty for the retailer is positioning. (Excuse the pun.) Where do you put it? The retailer may be missing marketing the tape, regardless of where he shelves the tape, because it is not an easily defined category.

Interviews also offer some erotic content. I imagine popular television stars like *Good Sex with Dr. Ruth* (Warner) will work in home video. There are several other sex interview shows but they do not have the mass awareness of a Dr. Ruth.

Romance

Romance is a new genre that has its roots in the success of the paperback novel form. It is eroticism for women. In the last year I have received about 15 proposals for creating a romance series. Upon first glance it would seem a natural extension of the publishing success of the romance form. But upon second glance, the Silhouette and Harlequin names have little recognition among video retailers. Consumers, yes; wholesalers and retailers, no. Bookstores, yes. The names are quite well known.

The problem comes with high production costs and pricing. To sell romance in bookstores or through mass merchants, the tapes would have to be sold at $29 or less. In the video stores they can be sold for $59 or maybe more if they are positioned like movies for rental. Because production values must be top-notch in order to successfully deliver in this genre (top stars, top writers, hit book titles, exotic locations, good cinematography and music), huge volumes of tapes must be sold to break even. Or, producers will need to find pay TV, broadcast, foreign or domestic theatrical partners. When you budget a

Romance Theatre
With Host
LOUIS JOURDAN
BAYOU ROMANCE
THE SHAME OF TWO UNTHINKABLE LOVE AFFAIRS... WHERE WOULD THEY END?

one-hour production (most romance stories are thin and cannot be stretched any longer) and come up with figures surpassing $500,000, wouldn't it make more sense to do a low-budget feature? Also, the genre doesn't appeal to the video retail buyer so you end up with high production costs and a very low-priced product.

In addition to the economic problems, the romance paperback sells at $1.95 or $2.25. For a small investment, it can be read and discarded. Would women actually buy romance videotape priced even as low as $9.95? Also by making a novel photographically explicit with real people, is the reader deprived of her own fantasies? Once you see the guy, is he really as attractive as you imagined? Although I am fascinated by the idea of adapting romance novels to tape, I couldn't make the economics of production and distribution work without putting together a multi-partnered structure combining pay TV, home video, book publishing and domestic and foreign television.

Prism Video is one of the first with romance videos. Their six feature-length romance films, acquired from Comworld, had very limited TV syndication exposure. They sell for $11.95. Karl/Lorimar announced eight romance films from L/A House Productions at a cost of $400,000 each. They too are priced at $11.95. Breakeven is about 60,000 units per title. It is an experiment worth watching.

Pseudo-exercise tapes such as the *Playmate Workout* (CBS/Fox) and *Eroticize* are for voyeurs; they'll do little more than exercise your eyeballs. Both have little verbal content and are predictably photographed. Perhaps that explains the success they have had in international markets as well.

Another sub-genre in the erotic category is compilations, such as *Sex in Cinema* (Karl/Lorimar), combining clips from erotic movies with high-brow narration, which somehow makes them *"socially redeemable."*

Party tapes, such as *Strip for Your Lover* and *Party Games*, suggest another erotic category. Then there is the ''*let's get naked*'' category. I have received numerous proposals from producers who want to take six nude models to exotic tropical locations to film for a few days. Regardless of how much fun it may be for the producer, his cast and investors, it's not what I would call a ''big idea.'' Today there are thousands of adult programs in the market that compete with the erotic genre. This tired idea just won't sell. Nevertheless it keeps getting pitched.

Exercise

There are more than 200 exercise tapes on the market, and more being released every month. With the phenomenal success of the *Jane Fonda Workout* series (Karl), virtually every home video company has released an exercise tape. For young to middle-aged women there is the *Jane Fonda Workout* (Karl). For middle-aged women there is *Raquel Welch: Total Beauty and Fitness* (Thorn/EMI), which has $1.5 million in sales. For middle-aged to older women there is the *Debbie Reynolds: Do It Debbie's Way* (Video Associates). Jane Fonda and Marie Osmond both have tapes for pregnant women. For men, there is *Body By Jake* (MCA), *Lyle Alzado: No Sweat* (Karl), and the *Armed Forces Workout* (Vestron). *The Playmate Workout* (CBS/Fox), *Eroticize* (Vestron), *Playgirl's Hunkercize* (Prism) are erotic tapes for every voyeur without any real instructional value. For the disabled, there is *Armchair Fitness* (CC-M), for dancers, *Aerobic Dancing* (MCA), for tap dancers, *Bonnie Franklin's Tap-Dance* (Karl). There are tapes for specific body parts, such as *Richard Simmons' Stomach Tape* (Karl), and *Firm Fannies* (Parade), and for general health there is *Pritikin's Promise* (Media Home Entertainment).

More than any other original programming genre, exercise tapes have demonstrated that original programs can be significant money-makers.

JANE FONDA'S
NEW
WORKOUT
JANE FONDA
WORKOUT
VHS
KARL·LORIMAR HOME VIDEO

Since 1985, the following videotapes have each grossed more than half a million dollars at the retail level. They are:

Title	Supplier	Unit Sales	Sugg. List	Est. Whlsl. $
Jane Fonda's Workout	Karl/Lorimar	515,000	$59.95	$ 19.5 mill.
Jane Fonda's Prime Time Workout	Karl/Lorimar	125,000	$39.95	3.3 mill.
Jane Fonda's Challenge Workout	Karl/Lorimar	80,000	$59.95	3 mill.
Do It Debbie's Way	Video Assoc.	75,000	$39.95	2 mill.
Every Day With Richard Simmons	Karl/Lorimar	40,000	$39.95	1 mill.
Raquel Welch: Total Beauty & Fitness	Thorn/EMI	35,000	$39.95	910,000
Jane Fonda's Workout for Pregnancy, Birth & Recovery	Karl/Lorimar	35,000	$59.95	1.3 mill.
Jazzercise	MCA	30,000	$39.95	840,000
Aerobic Dancing	MCA	20,000	$39.95	560,000
Body by Jake	MCA	15,000	$39.95	420,000

(Source: Knowledge Industry Publications.)

The success of the Jane Fonda tapes has propelled the entire exercise phenomenon. In fact, the 10 top-selling exercise tapes have sold a million cassettes combined (U.S.) and have grossed more than $32 million for their program suppliers. This is even more staggering when one stops to consider that there has been no theatrical window or exposure of these tapes. Jane Fonda alone has generated more than $27 million.

THORN EMI
VIDEO
"It's my way to stay completely in shape."
–RAQUEL WELCH
RAQUEL
TOTAL BEAUTY AND FITNESS

Exercise tapes do have the advantage that they can be distributed not only through the traditional outlets, but through mail order, mass merchandisers, and alternative distribution channels like department stores, sporting goods stores and health spas.

Raquel Welch's tape has done terrific business as well. This tape was carefully and expertly promoted by Raquel and accompanied by superb posters and point-of-purchase displays. Racquel's numerous personal appearances in video stores and bookstores further expanded the public's awareness of the tape.

The star value in the exercise field cannot be overlooked. Nor can the various tapes that are targeted to specific age groups. There is even a tape for children, called *Mousercize* (Disney). Smart producers may find other niches in the marketplace and employ stars who would tour and promote their tapes.

The beauty of exercise tapes is that they can be produced very inexpensively, not including talent fees. Jane Fonda was the first to expand on her tapes with a more advanced exercise program. The producers of the Debbie Reynolds tape decided to make their tape easier than Jane Fonda's when they realized the older market had been neglected. It paid off.

Repeatability is important. Exercise enthusiasts want to view the tape again and again while they work out. (This may not be true for men who tend to exercise outside of the house or in the gym—an obvious warning to producers about making tapes for men.) Consequently, producers should make their tapes repeatable when they design their programs. Be careful not to have too many non-exercise breaks or informational sections. Otherwise the tape will become boring on subsequent playings. The non-repeatable sections should come at the beginning or end of the tape. *The 20-Minute Workout* (Vestron) has three 20-minute sessions on one tape. This way a viewer can play any of the sequences and not tire of the tape so quickly. Exercise proponents (mostly

:20 MINUTE WORKOUT
THREE COMPLETE WORKOUTS FOR THE PRICE OF ONE!

JANE FONDA'S
PRIME TIME
WORKOUT
$39.95
SUGGESTED RETAIL PRICE
VHS
JANE FONDA WORKOUT
KARL HOME VIDEO

ARMED
FORCES
WORKOUT
THE NATIONAL PHENOMENON
NOW ON HOME VIDEO!

producers) claim that as people tire of Fonda and other programs they will search for new exercise tapes. Exercise tapes have also been popular because they offer exercise at non-scheduled times. You do not have to go to a class or even leave your home. Also, a videotape is economical; it costs about the same as two or three exercise classes.

There have been, in fact, so many exercise tapes that critics have designed their own rating scale of one to five for warmup, aerobics, strength, flexibility, progression, cool-down, appearance, with an overall score for the tape itself. Producers should keep these qualities in mind. Pay as much attention to the substance as the sizzle. The Mercury News rated *Jane Fonda's Prime Time Workout* (Karl), first; *Richard Simmons' Family Fitness* (Karl), second; and *The Armed Forces Workout* (Vestron), third in the qualities listed above.

Muscle Motion, starring the men from Chippendale's (Media Home Entertainment), a popular male stripper nightclub, gained significant attention when a physical exercise teacher was fired for showing the tape to her Phys. Ed. class. The mini-scandal helped sell tapes. How do you promote your tape in an already overcrowded field? If you can answer this question, then your exercise idea may have merit.

How-To

More than any other original program category, how-tos offer the greatest opportunity for subject matter. There are virtually hundreds of possibilities. This genre also provides the easiest entry for independent producers. How-to books have been successful; there is no reason (perhaps other than price) that how-to tapes will not also prove successful. For many subjects, a videotape can be more useful as a teaching tool than the printed page. You can show—how to do it.

BREAKING
with the
MIGHTY POPPALOTS
Learn
step by step…
with the
country's best
breakdance
team!

Virtually every home video company has released at least one how-to tape. Examples of successful how-to tapes are the *Jane Fonda Workout* (Karl/Lorimar), *Raquel: Total Beauty and Fitness* (Thorn/EMI) at $39.95, *Wok Before You Run* (Embassy, a Chinese cooking tape), *Strong Kids, Safe Kids* (Paramount), which sold some 30,000 units at $29.95, and *Breakin' with the Mighty Poppalots* (Vestron) at $39.95, which has sold well internationally. There isn't a subject that hasn't already been put on videotape. Tapes can be found on parenting, beauty, health, fun learning, music, sports, language, dance, hobbies, diet, sex, safety, selfdefense, finance, cooking, education, home repair, gardening, travel, and so on.

Today tapes range in price from a low of $6.99 to $89.95. (This does not include training tapes, which are sold in the business and industry market on video for up to $2,500.) The subjects can be highly specialized. For example, 3-M has launched a line of high-priced $89.95 fly-fishing tapes. Some video retail stores sell tapes, but mostly these how-to tapes are sold by mail order, direct response magazine ads, and in specialty outlets such as bookshops, sports stores, hardware stores, and health clubs.

Producers of how-to tapes should first study the market and explore what tapes already exist. Does the world need another tape on landscape irrigation? Producers may wish to consider whether the tape can provide better and more useful information as a video than in book form. For example, a how-to tape on basketball may not be practical if you have to take the VHS machine and monitor outside to the hoop for playback. Reference books fare poorly, in my opinion, as videotapes. A first-aid book might be very valuable when a child spills turpentine in its eye, but to try to access the same information quickly on a videotape in an emergency is out of the question. It's not really a practical or useful storage form for information that has to be accessed quickly. There may come a time when interactive videodiscs could provide this rapid access and be a perfect medium for reference material.

LISA SLIWA'S
COMMON SENSE
DEFENSE
SHE'S A HIGH-FASHION MODEL BY DAY... A GUARDIAN ANGEL BY NIGHT.
GUARDIAN ANGELS

One does not have to travel far to find ideas for how-tos. Books provide an excellent source. So do existing how-to television shows. For your program to compete with thousands already made, the information must have value—it must be able to be played more than once or be so hard to come by (such as a recluse chairman of the board who gives a speech on entrepreneurship) that the tape has value. A successful tape needs to employ a credible host or spokesperson, be well made, have a *''hook''* and still be priced low enough so that someone would want to purchase it!

As prices drop below $14.95, it is quite likely that instructional tapes in shorter lengths will be produced. Once again, the information would have to be valuable enough or *''collectible''* enough for someone to want to own it. Today how-to tapes will not be sold in great volumes through the traditional video stores but rather through mass merchandisers, convenience and drugstores, bookstores, direct marketing and other outlets that are sale- rather than rental-oriented. Esquire (through Kartes) has recently released a well-made, well-packaged and well-promoted six-tape fitness series titled *Esquire: Great Body*. The 30-minute tape will sell for $14.95 through mass markets, supermarkets and drugstores. This suggests a possible trend in how-to marketing.

Games

Only a dozen original programs have yet to appear in the game category. The most successful home video game to date has been Parker Brother's *Clue,* which was based on the popular board game. *Clue* sold more than 300,000 units at $39.95. This was predated by programs that were less successful such as *Money Hunt* from Karl Video, released mid-1984. This program is a detective story with clues that led the viewer to a cash prize. About the same time, Vestron released *Treasure* at $39.95. This was a film about a young girl's search for a stolen gold horse. It also was the viewer's search for an actual gold horse buried

TREASURE
IN SEARCH OF THE GOLDEN HORSE
WIN
A PRIZE OF
$500,000
Film by
Sheldon Renan.
Puzzle by
Dr. Crypton.
Original
Soundtrack
by Jesse
Frederick.
A complete set of rules is included on this videocassette.

somewhere in the Continental U.S. and yet to be found. The clever person who studies the clues within the tape and actually digs up the gold horse (which weighs some three pounds) will keep it and receive a cash prize of $500,000.

Other games on video are *The Gold Key* (Embassy), *Casino Gambling* (Karl), *Rich Little's VCR Charade Game* and *Party Games for Adults Only* (MCA).

Video retailers, however, will be less than enthusiastic about renting or selling home video games that have oversized boxes or movable pieces. Stand-alone home video games packaged in standard sizes mean the retailer will have no problem finding a place for it on his already limited shelf. However, the success of Clue and other home video games that have sold well in toy stores points to an emerging genre that could continue to generate sales as the distribution outlets open up. Producers should beware—at this juncture in the video business any supplemental material provided with a tape is quickly lost or discarded in the video retail store when it is rented.

In late 1987 inexpensive interactive VCR games will be introduced using a control box that allows the VCR to operate like a videodisc so that viewers can make interactive moves via the television set. The inventor of the control box is in discussions with Simon and Schuster, Lucasfilm and Warner regarding software, and Parker Bros., Milton Bradley and Coleco on the hardware. As the market expands, one can expect to see more games of all kinds become a staple genre on the home video scene.

Environmental

"Video wallpaper" are non-narrative, often purely visual tapes of waterfalls, rivers, streams, coral banks, aquariums, fireplaces and country roads. These are electronic concept pieces (real cheap to

produce) and are put on the television screen in the same way that some records are played as background music. They have not been terribly successful in the U.S. (other than the well-produced Windham Hill series which reportedly sold about 30,000 units). This form is primarily a gimmick.

Japan, however, loves this form. One of the most successful environmental tapes of all time was sold in Japan. It showed one of those hideous lizards with puffy gill-cheeks running upright on its two hind legs at breakneck speed across a desert. Fusion jazz was the accompanying music track. Its success had more to do with the fact that this lizard was frequently seen on television commercials for beer or sake and was something of a cult figure. Needless to say, there have been no environmental best sellers since. They appeal to an extremely limited audience.

There are approximately 30 of these in the marketplace. They are distributed by Environmental Video, Pacific Arts, Video Naturals and Paramount.

Business and Industry

One segment of the non-theatrical market—the business and industry market—has prospered in recent years. This market is highly specialized and primarily offers training tapes to business concerns. Films or tapes are sold or leased at extremely high prices ($500 to $2,500) to the Fortune 1000 companies and other large or medium-sized businesses. The information contained on these tapes is of great value to the buyer and often replaces expensive in-house seminars or lectures by high-priced speakers. Many corporations produce their own training and educational materials. Like the book business, the time will come when business tapes will be available in home video. Any well-stocked bookstore has a business section. As the market develops, there will undoubtedly be a plethora of business audio and videotapes covering

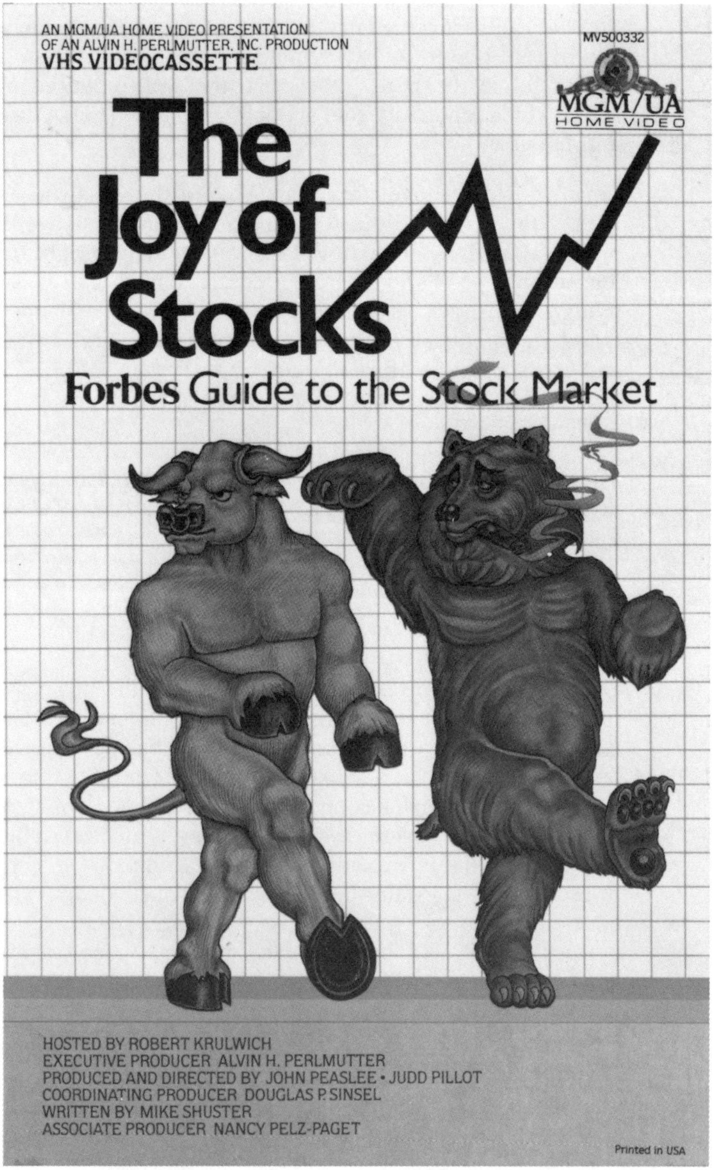
AN MGM/UA HOME VIDEO PRESENTATION
OF AN ALVIN H. PERLMUTTER, INC. PRODUCTION
VHS VIDEOCASSETTE
MV500332
MGM/UA
HOME VIDEO
The Joy of Stocks
Forbes Guide to the Stock Market
HOSTED BY ROBERT KRULWICH
EXECUTIVE PRODUCER ALVIN H. PERLMUTTER
PRODUCED AND DIRECTED BY JOHN PEASLEE • JUDD PILLOT
COORDINATING PRODUCER DOUGLAS P. SINSEL
WRITTEN BY MIKE SHUSTER
ASSOCIATE PRODUCER NANCY PELZ-PAGET
Printed in USA

popular business themes such as personal finance, estate planning, how to buy real estate, the stock market, income taxes, etc. Initially these tapes will not be sold through the traditional video retailer, nor through the book stores, but through direct mail at high prices. (Bookstores tend to only stock tapes at $29 or under with few exceptions.) Like every other form of programming, a strong title, a well-known business personality and a credible sponsor or publication umbrella will be necessary to make significant sales.

In 1985 the business and industry market had gross revenues of about $500 million annually. These revenues came primarily from sales to corporations. There will come a time when the prices of these tapes will fall for the mass market but probably not any time soon. They are too profitable. A supplier would have to sell about 50 tapes to consumers to equal the one sale he presently has to make through corporate clients.

CBS is currently one of the leaders in this field. It has released 60- to 90-minute titles such as Naisbitt's *Megatrends,* McCormack's *What They Don't Teach You at Harvard Business School, Presentation Excellence* with Walter Cronkite, Blanchard's *Putting the One-Minute Manager To Work, Bill Cosby on Prejudice,* Dyer's *Your Erroneous Zones* and Cohen's *Persuasive Negotiating.* These titles are sold in both 1/2-inch and 3/4-inch video formats as well as in 16mm. Prices range from $400 to $1,200, depending on the format. *The One-Minute Manager* ($1,250), *Megatrends* ($1,350), and *A Passion for Excellence* ($795) have sold more than 10,000 units.

CBS/Fox claims that the business and industry market has seen a 70% annual compounded growth rate. The company currently ranks in the top 10 (in a field of 20 or more). Many of these tapes have accompanying workbooks and study materials.

In Search of Excellence has been the best seller of all time with 8,000 units sold at $495 over 14 months. Based on a phenomenally successful book and broadcast on PBS, the program was widely known and well-regarded. The program was self-distributed by its producers, John Nathan and Sam Tyler.

Major corporations can easily justify the high cost of these tapes. Paying an author or top business expert to speak could easily cost $10,000. A tape is cheap by comparison and can be circulated through management at its convenience as well. CBS claims that a good title is one that generates $2 million in sales (1,600 units at $1,200 each). Star titles bring in $3 million (2,500 units), and a $4 million sale (3,300 units) is spectacular. Royalties to the writers are in the range of 25% and often carry escalation clauses. Budgets can range from $200,000 for *Megatrends* to $250,000 for *Presentation Excellence*. Many of the programs are produced in-house.

While it is difficult to get a fix on the overall annual revenues of the business and industry market, the big picture may look something like this. Sales to business and government were $250 million in 1983 and $285 million in 1984. Video accounted for more than 85% of sales with 16mm film making up the difference. The school and library market (also considered the non-theatrical market) was about $45 million and rose to $50 million from 1983 to 1984. In 1983 video was in about 31% of all schools. Today there are 64,744 schools with at least one VCR, said Jeanne Hayes, president of Denver-based Quality Education Data Inc. By the end of the year the VCR will be in nearly 80% of all schools. VCRs are cheaper than most 16mm films, and video software is considerably cheaper than film prints.

The superstar companies producing and distributing for the business and government market are: Deltak (Prentice Hall) with $75 million in gross revenues; Xerox Learning Systems (now Learning International), $50 million; and Advanced Systems Inc. at $40 million annually. There are approximately 20 other companies that have sales in excess of $2 million a year. There are McGraw-Hill's three companies (Edutronics, Traytex, CRM) with $15 million in gross revenues, Time-Life Video with $12 million, BNA Communications with $12 million, Sterling Institute with $6 million, and American Management Association with $2.5 million. It is estimated that the size of the new video business and industry market is nearly $600 million today.

Children's Video

Children's video programming is, by far, the fastest-growing genre in original programming. Children's titles are estimated to account for some 10%-15% of the overall home video revenues. With retail prices falling and alternative retail outlets expanding, children's programming will soon become one of the most profitable segments of the video market. By 1990 it could account for as much as 25% of total sales. Total 1985 sales were about $100 million.

One of the advantages that children's programming has over most other forms of programming is that it is automatically repeatable; children enjoy watching the same program again and again. (Some studies say kids will watch a tape 30 to 50 times!) Rather than rent tapes again and again, parents buy the tape at prices between $9.95 and $29.95.

Video dealers purchase children's video because it rents continuously. It has a long shelf life. In the same way that children want their favorite books read again and again, they also want to view their favorite cassettes more than once.

With feature films there is a 90% rental to 10% sales ratio. More recently the ratio has shifted to 80/20, but with children's product, more than 30% of all revenues are from sales and growing all the time. The increase is due to the fact that there are more and more retail outlets carrying children's programming. Toy stores like Toys 'R' Us, Child

THE ADVENTURES
OF
The Little Prince
AWARD WINNER
nea Recommended by the National Education Association

World, and Woolworth's all carry children's product. Manufacturers are selling tapes at Toy Fair and the American Booksellers Association (ABA).

Walt Disney Home Video has the largest share of the children's video market, 60% or more. Vestron's Children's Video Library (CVL) also holds a large share. This is happening because the baby boomers are having babies and want to control what their children are watching. In addition, retail prices, which had been as high as $79, are now falling to $19.95 and even $9.95. In the video retail store, which buys tape for rentals, sales tend to stop after two or three volumes of the same title. In the emerging sell-through market of toy stores and mass merchandisers, the same resistance does not occur because consumers seem to be collecting tape series and will buy volume after volume if their kids liked the first.

As with every successful business, entrepreneurs rush in. Nearly every major supplier of programming has jumped in, creating a glut of product. Consumers and retailers are both very confused as to what they should buy. Programs that are the most successful are the well-known licensed characters familiar to kids from Saturday morning like The Care Bears, the Hulk, Robot Man, My Little Pony, Rainbow Brite, Hugga-Bunch and others.

CBS/Fox programs received gold videos (20,000 units or $800,000 in sales) with the children's titles *Snow White and the Seven Dwarfs, Sleeping Beauty, Rapunzel, Beauty and the Beast, Goldilocks and the Three Bears,* and *Tale of the Frog Prince.*

Worldvision says children's video sales account for 50% of its business. Most of its programs are from its massive Hanna-Barbera library. Prism bought 213 half-hour TV programs featuring Marvel super heroes. The programs are packaged in boxes designed by Marvel comic artists and are sold for $19.95. A pre-sold audience of 15 million Marvel comic book readers exists for the tapes.

VOLUME IV
CHALLENGE OF THE GOBOTS™
Fully — Animated
FORCED ALLIANCE
FROM HANNA-BARBERA PRODUCTIONS, INC.
AND Tonka CORPORATION

Besides highly visible programs featuring licensed characters, other forms of original children's programming are beginning to emerge. Paramount released *Strong Kids, Safe Kids* with the TV star Henry "the Fonz" Winkler: a tape that children and parents watch together to help prevent child abuse. In a similar vein, Disney released *Too Smart for Strangers* about the importance of self-defense and safety. *It's Your Birthday with Rainbow Brite* is an original program from Vestron that is quasi-interactive and is viewed at kids' birthday parties. The tape invites kids to sing and dance along with Rainbow Brite (while parents enjoy a respite from the party, leaving chaperoning to a video surrogate). The tape also comes with an activity/coloring book.

Other programs have included value-added premiums with the tapes although some dealers have found difficulty with the unwieldly non-standard-size packages. Vestron found success when it packaged *Benji* with a stuffed dog of the same name. Undoubtedly we will see more toy and book premiums accompany videotapes in the future. These will find more success in mass, department and toy store outlets because they are accustomed to this kind of packaging.

We will also see more programs that call on the child viewer for participation. Recent interactive programs include MCA's *Be Somebody with Mr. T* and *Disney's Animal Quiz.*

Some interactive tapes fall into the "fun-learning" or educational category. MGM/UA released *You Can Do It,* starring Shari Lewis and her puppets teaching magic.

Spinnaker Software Corporation is the largest supplier of educational computer software. In 1985 it introduced a line of educational videos priced at $19.97, which included a 40-page workbook. The tapes were cleverly packaged and titled. Examples are *Math: Add Ventures of the Time Taxi, Math: Close Encounters of the Math Kind,* and *Reading: Readers of the Lost Alphabet.* The tapes featured Muppet-like characters teaching math and reading skills to the 5 to 8 and 7 to 10 age

Joe Camp's
Benji
IN BENJI'S VERY OWN CHRISTMAS STORY
Special Bonus Program: The Phenomenon of Benji
Produced and directed by JOE CAMP • Screenplay by JOE CAMP
Starring BENJI • CYNTHIA SMITH • PATSY GARRETT • RON MOODY

groups. They are somewhat interactive because at certain points in the programs kids go to the workbooks. Although the tapes are only 40 minutes long, they provide up to five hours of education and entertainment. Spinnaker sold about 50,000 units per title. Production budget was in the $150,000 range per tape.

Most children's programmers agree that educational and instructional programming will be the wave of the future. There is a general distrust of programming that is based on toy or television characters. Moreover, parents want the tapes to provide some educational value and are willing to pay for it. Children now spend 30 hours per week watching television. Parents would like to see some of this time used for mind-enhancing or educational purposes. When Vestron released the *National Geographic Video* series, it was surprised to find that parents collected the programs for themselves and their children. And the children watched the programs repeatedly like other forms of programming.

For parents who are concerned about how to differentiate between high-quality programming and drek, there is the *Children's Video Report* (Woolworth Building, Suite 3715, 223 Broadway, New York, NY 10279), a newsletter with information and essays about video programming. Like anything else, poor-quality programming will be sold in a hit-and-run fashion and quality programming will prevail.

Programs for children are particularly expensive to produce. Animation is extremely expensive. Some producers have found innovative methods to cut costs. Western Publishing produced a series of tapes that are little more than book pages being turned, read and videotaped. Books are *"slow-scanned"* (the camera pans over the pages) and a narrator simply reads the story. The series uses Golden Book stories and is promoted as *"Story Books Brought to Life."* Each tape has three to five stories per tape running three to 10 minutes each. The packaging is excellent and the tapes were promoted with a million dollar campaign. It paid off. The first series of eight tapes sold more than 1.6 million tapes at $9.97. Some of the tapes included more sophisticated slow-scan techniques with dissolves and minor special effects. Production costs were in the $75,000 to $100,000 range per tape.

Successes like this have encouraged many video manufacturers to go into the lucrative world of children's programming but often find it difficult to compete with premier names like Disney Home Video. In 1984 and 1985, Disney released limited gold editions of some of its major titles, such as *Life With Mickey, From Pluto With Love, An Officer and a Duck, The World According to Goofy,* and sold more than 600,000 cassettes at $29.95. Studies estimate that by 1990 more than 25 million families with children will own at least one VCR. It is evident that there will be many opportunities for producers to produce original children's programming in the years to come. The parents who now have younger children are very concerned about what their children watch. Video tapes give them the ability to monitor their children's television viewing. Consumers will look for high-quality product with recognizable names.

An obvious place to look for recognizable characters is with toy companies, book publishers and television syndicators. Toy companies such as Mattel, Coleco and Hasbro have already produced numerous tapes based on their characters. However, most major product will already have been earmarked for home video release prior to production. Most product that has already been broadcast has already been licensed by manufacturers. Opportunities will continue to exist for independent producers to create original programs with well-known celebrities such as Henry Winkler's *Strong Kids, Safe Kids.*

Behind Disney, the three leading manufacturers of children's programming are Family Home Entertainment, Vestron Video and RCA/Columbia.

C. J. Kettler, vice-president of Vestron's Children's Video Library says, "By utilizing a well-known character, you capitalize on the

The Care Bears Movie
The Samuel Goldwyn Company presents
"THE CARE BEARS MOVIE"
Introducing The Care Bear Cousins
A Nelvana Production
with MICKEY ROONEY as the voice of Mr. Cherrywood
Title Song by CAROLE KING Songs by JOHN SEBASTIAN
Producers: Michael Hirsh, Patrick Loubert and Clive Smith
Directed by Arna Selznick

market impression originated by the toy manufacturers and program producers.'' Regarding the advertising and promotional budget for the film, she says, ''*The Care Bears Movie* has exceeded $24 million in box office rentals. That sum, combined with the $1 billion in retail sales of Care Bears merchandise, gives the title enormous value in home video.''

Of all tapes sold, it is estimated that children's video represents 10%-15%. Popular properties have included the *Care Bears, Thunder Cats, Transformers, Rainbow Brite, My Little Pony, Ziggy, Voltron—Defender of the Universe,* and others.

Disney entered the children's exercise area with a tape geared for 3- to 8-year-olds titled *Mousercize,* priced at $39.95 with only marginal results. ABC Video/Karl Lorimar released a *Mary Lou Retton* exercise tape at $29.95 with disappointing results. The big question: *Do kids really want to exercise?*

If producers can't get a licensed character, television star, or well-known book character for their programs, they still may be able to acquire public domain children's book titles and produce animated or live action stories. Classic stories appeal to parents who may wish to build a classic video library for their children and to have them avoid the violence of Saturday morning animations.

As children's programming grows in popularity, there will be tremendously exciting opportunities for creative producers with a strong ability to develop informative and entertaining programs for children.

Music Video

Music videos have generated more enthusiasm in the past few years than perhaps any other form of non-feature programming but have been somewhat disappointing compared to the expectations of manufacturers *and producers alike. The remarkable success of Making Michael Jackson's Thriller* (Vestron Video), which sold over a million videos worldwide, led many to dream of similar sales figures which, so far, have been unobtainable. Of the 26 all-time top-selling video cassettes, all have included major stars. Combined, they total 2.4 million units with estimated wholesale revenues at nearly $45 million.

Other major hits have included Prince's *Purple Rain* (Warner Home Video), a feature film priced to sell at $29. Initial shipments were 475,000 units. *We Are The World* (RCA/Columbia, $14.95), 175,000 units; *Lionel Ritchie* (RCA/Columbia, $14.95), 125,000 units; *BandAid* (Vestron Video $9.95), 120,000 units; and *Rolling Stones Video Rewind* (Vestron Video, $29.95), 110,000 units. These top six titles, including *Thriller,* account for about 67% of all sales and 64% of the wholesale revenue. When you move to the remaining 20 titles on the best-selling list, the numbers fall off dramatically, with most selling between 25,000 and 80,000 units, at prices ranging from $16.95 to $39.95 generally. Most manufacturers say that music videos have not sold as well as was anticipated a year or two ago, and average sales are between 5,000 and 10,000 units.

There are several reasons for this less-than-anticipated sales volume. First, there is an overabundance of free music videos appearing on *MTV, VH-1,* the major networks and more than a hundred other television programs. Second, the prices of videos for teens are high and many do not even own a VCR. Music videos are being marketed to a group that doesn't even own the equipment to play them! Third, most succesful tapes have been with major stars who attract an affluent audience. And fourth, the videos are often not released until long after the record has cooled. Pop music is a time-sensitive business and videotapes that are not released concurrent with the album will suffer. Vestron's release of Pete Townshend's *White City* was out at the same time as the album and cross-promoted. Both were best sellers.

Like other original program genres, music can be broken down into

Good Vibrations!
AN AMERICAN BAND
The Beach Boys
For The First Time – The True Story Behind The Legendary Group That Created The California Sound
PG
PARENTAL GUIDANCE RECOMMENDED
Hi-Fi STEREO
DIRECT FROM THEATRICAL RELEASE
RELEASE DATE COINCIDES WITH AUSTRALIAN TOUR FEB 15 – 24.
THEATRICAL SIZE POSTER AND SUN VISORS AVAILABLE
• NSW (02) 908 4333 or 008 022561
• VIC (03) 690 3022 • SA (08) 332 9233
• QLD (07) 369 7388 • WA (09) 381 4055

sub-genres: historical compilations that use old footage of performances and interviews as source material, performances and concerts, concept (non-narrative) music videos, story or long-form music movies that use traditional movie plot structures. Creatively all these forms offer great possibilities. To produce them expediently and inexpensively is another matter. For producers working outside the record companies, many will find it very difficult to produce music programs. The reason is that record companies own the music rights—the synchronization and master recording licenses—and therefore control the music product. Leaders in music are RCA/Columbia, CBS/Fox, Warner Music Video and Sony Video. Independent video producers who are not affiliated with a record company must pay very high costs for music licenses from record companies. In addition, the top stars are accustomed to high fees, escalating costs far beyond what can realistically be recouped from most low-priced music video product.

Some have produced programs that require little cooperation from record companies or they acquire music licenses from smaller record companies who do not produce their own music videos. Pacific Art's *Say Amen Somebody* was a gospel tribute. Vestron acquired the rights to individual music videos for the compilation *Comedy Music Videos.*

Compilations of vintage music clips, with the exception of the *Compleat Beatles* (MGM/UA), *Girl Groups* (MGM/UA), *The Doors: Dance on Fire* (MCA) and *The Beach Boys: An American Band* (Vestron), have fared poorly in the marketplace. Producers must acquire all underlying rights to the material, such as film footage, performance clearances and music synch rights. It may be necessary to acquire as many as nine different rights on one piece of music film footage. While the individual rights may not in themselves be expensive, by the time everyone is paid it can cost up to $30,000 for a clip depending on its perceived value by all the rights holders. With costs escalating like this, recoupment could be deferred to the day when they open up those pearly gates.

PETE TOWNSHEND
$29.95
suggested retail price
White City
THE MUSIC MOVIE

Producers wishing to make music videos stand a better chance by working directly with the major record companies, who have their own home video labels. They could also develop alternative long-form music or dramatic programs for superstar performers. This way, name talent could be obtained and producers could circumvent the record companies' control. Would this create a type of product that retailers and consumers would want to buy? After all, the music talent would be acting—not playing music. It's doubtful, but perhaps too early to tell.

Most home video program distributors feel that unless a video is performed by a major artist who is on a national tour and who has a major hit on the charts with frequent airings on MTV, it will be difficult to sell more than 10,000 cassettes. As prices fall, however, and approach that of albums, it may be possible to sell more units. But still, production costs will remain high and only sales in great volume will make up for price reductions. As prices are reduced to $19.95, $9.95 and lower, mass merchandisers such as Woolworth's, K mart, Target Stores and others will enter the music video business and increase the number of units sold.

Even major artists such as Tina Turner, David Bowie, Duran Duran, and Iron Maiden, who have sold about 25,000 units each, would average sales of only 1.4 cassettes per retail outlet. Sales such as these have made record stores and video retailers wary of music video. In addition, many suppliers and manufacturers must guarantee return privileges of cassettes that don't sell, making them even more cautious about even acquiring *time-sensitive* music product. There was a time in the record industry when an album may have shipped "platinum" but returned *"gold."* Those who remember the economic demise of the record business don't want to see history repeat itself.

Sony Video Software has released about 80 music titles, 50 of which are short-form videos (usually four) at $16.95. Producers are reporting little

LIBERACE LIVE
Baldwin
EXECUTIVE DIRECTOR: SEYMOUR HELLER
PRODUCED BY: DEREK BOULTON
ASSOCIATE PRODUCER: JOHN FISHER
STAGED AND PRODUCED BY: RAY ARNETT
MUSICAL DIRECTOR: BO AYARS   ORCHESTRA LEADER: DAVID NOLAN
CONDUCTED BY: DAVID SNELL   EDITED FOR VIDEO BY: DAVID LEVINE
PRODUCTION BY: STEWART MORRIS   MARKETED BY: PROMARK

DICK CLARK'S
Best Of
BANDSTAND
RATE-A-RECORD
BILL HALEY, BUDDY HOLLY, CHUBBY CHECKER, THE EVERLY BROTHERS, JERRY LEE LEWIS, THE BIG BOPPER AND MORE!
ORIGINAL PERFORMANCES— NOW AVAILABLE EXCLUSIVELY ON VIDEO!

or no advances for their programs and small royalties, but all expect business to improve over the next few years.

Producers note: *It is important to select artists with longevity rather than flash-in-the-pan music acts to realize a long-term profit.* Record companies will still release most of their own videos, which are made primarily for promotional purposes. Any income from music video sales is gravy and helps to recoup production and promotion costs.

Regardless of the difficulty in clearing music rights, dealing with egocentric talent, and producing music videos, it is clear that they will continue to exist as a popular original program form. Markets will expand. Teenagers will someday have their own VCRs. Producers interested in this genre should make friends with music publishers and record companies before designing programs that will be thwarted by rights holders.

Biographies/Personalities

Biographies are really a sub-set of documentary or dramatic forms, but since there are more than 50 currently in the marketplace they can be thought of as a genre.

Biographies or personality-based programs already fill one of the requirements for successful original programs: They have a promotable personality. Obviously a biography on an unknown person will have little appeal.

There are a number of smaller distributors handling biographies. They have entered the arena because the competition for features is fierce and they find it easier to acquire other forms of programming. Few biographies have sold more than 3,000 or 4,000 units, but for small companies that's really OK. Bios are distributed by companies such as RKI, Monterey, Mastervision, Video Yesteryear, Blackhawk, MCA, USA, Media, Key, Karl, Prism and Vestron. Biographies use

EMBASSY HOME ENTERTAINMENT
The Love Goddesses
"An olympus of 39 dimpled deities" —TIME
"FIRST RATE" —NEW YORKER
"EXCELLENT" —NEW YORK TIMES
"FASCINATING" —SATURDAY REVIEW
from the Janus Collection

THE PRINCE AND
PRINCESS OF WALES
Talking Personally
With Alastair Burnet
This video is produced with
the co-operation of Their Royal Highnesses
The Prince and Princess of Wales.
ITN

compiled clips from famous movies or documentary footage of the characters' lives. Some sample titles are: *The James Dean Story* (MCA), *Rita Hayworth: the Love Goddess* (USA), *Reverend Jesse Jackson* (MCA), *Roy Rogers: Champion of the People* (VCA), *The Legend of Valentino* (Prism), *The Prince & Princess of Wales: Talking Personally* (Vestron).

Cultural

Cultural programming encompasses dance, theater, art and the performing arts. It generally covers the more highbrow subject areas. Leading distributors are Kultur, Mastervision, Corinth, RKO, Monterey, MGM/UA, Coffee Table, and Simon and Schuster. Examples of some titles are: *Chekhov Treasury* (in three volumes,Mastervision), *Cyrano de Bergerac* (Corinth), *The Gin Game, Sweeney Todd* (both RKO), *Ibsen's A Doll House* (MGM/UA), *The Tragedy of King Richard II* (Kultur) and *Jewel in the Crown* (Simon and Schuster). Thorn/EMI/HBO has one of the more extensive cultural lines with 60 ballet and opera cassettes with a permanent display case for $39.95.

Many cultural programs have had a previous existence on PBS, the BBC or other foreign television networks. Unfortunately, reusuary rights also exist on dramas and musical performances and payments to the various guilds are required for home video exploitation. These rights could cost as much as $60,000 per program depending on the number of actors, musicians and music clearances required, so, for the producer, it could be a very expensive proposition. Furthermore, sales of cultural videos have, for the most part, been less than 2,000 units per title even though many of these have sold at high prices. As the VCR base expands, there will be more cultural programming released.

Cat On A
Hot Tin Roof
A Showtime Entertainment/American Playhouse presenta
An International Television Group/KCET production
JESSICA LANGE TOMMY LEE JONES
TENNESSEE WILLIAMS'
CAT ON A HOT TIN ROOF
Starring RIP TORN KIM STANLEY PENNY FULLER DAVID
Executive Producer LOU LaMONTE
Producer PHYLIS GELLER
Directed by JACK HOFSISS

Dance

There are more than 60 dance videos on the market today. Leading distributors are Pacific Arts, Corinth, Mastervision, American Home, Kultur, Thorn/EMI/HBO, CBS, and MGM/UA. Titles include major ballets with several versions of each being recorded, as well as more modern experimental dance programs. Examples are: *Backstage at the Kirov, Anna Karenina, The Bolshoi Ballet, Carmen, Coppelia, Catherine Wheel, Giselle, Sleeping Beauty: The Kirov Ballet.*

Language

There are approximately 20 language videocassettes in the marketplace currently. The releases have come from Mastervision, Karl, CBS and Rizzoli. Few of the cassettes have sold more than 2,000 each. However, this type of programming has an *"evergreen"* quality to it and will see slow but steady sales for many years to come.

Sports

Hundreds of sports tapes on every discipline imaginable have already been released. Many are from small companies but some large companies as well have participated in the sports genre. The following list represents many of the sports tapes released to date, along with representative distributors. They are:

Subject	**Number**	**Distributor**
Aviation/Flying	20	Blackhawk
Baseball	36	RCA, Sybervision, CBS
Basketball	10	RMI, Embassy
Bowling	4	Sybervision

hi-fi
MONO
EMBASSY HOME ENTERTAINMENT®
BASEBALL
The Pete Rose Way
LEARN BASEBALL FROM A LIVING LEGEND!
ALL TIME HIT LEADER
HOLDER OF MORE RECORDS THAN ANY OTHER MODERN PLAYER
THE ONLY ALL STAR NAMED TO FIVE DIFFERENT POSITIONS
NATIONAL LEAGUE MOST VALUABLE PLAYER
ATHLETE OF THE DECADE — 1970's

Wrestling
RINGMASTERS
THE GREAT AMERICAN BASH
RIC FLAIR vs. NIKITA KOLOFF
TULLY BLANCHARD vs. "THE AMERICAN DREAM" DUSTY RHODES
THE ROAD WARRIORS vs. IVAN KOLOFF & KRUSHER KHRUSCHEV
MAGNUM T.A. vs. KAMALA THE UGANDAN GIANT
Produced by JOHN J. BURZICHELLI
Co-producer JEFFERY J. ODDO
Associate Producers: PETER KING · CRAIG PETERS

THE WINNING EDGE
JOHN McENROE/IVAN LENDL
PRIVATE LESSONS WITH THE PROS
Starring JOHN McENROE and IVAN LENDL
Based on an original concept
by John Yandell

Boxing	4	Blackhawk
Fishing	30	Sportsman
Football	50	NFL
Golf	30	Sybervision, CBS, Golf Digest, Sports World, RCA
Horses	7	RMI
Hunting	15	Sportsman
Karate	3	
Olympics	10	Embassy, USA, Continental, Classic
Sailing	40	Gravity Sports, RMI, Sea TV
Self-Defense	10	Karl, Paramount, MPI, American Home, Increase, Active, Vestron
Skiing	20	RMI, RCA, Karl, Monterey, Gravity Sports, Sybervision
Sports History	20	NFL, USA
Sports Star Profiles	30	Great Sports Legends
Tennis	20	Sportsworld, RMI, Pacific Arts, USA, Vestron
Track and Field	12	RCA, Media, RMI
Wrestling	15	Vestron, Coliseum Ocean, Active, Gravity Sports

Until 1986 Continental Video's *1984 Summer Olympics* was the best-selling sports title. It has been replaced by NFL Films Video's *Chicago Bears Shuffle*, which sold 120,000 units. Polk Bros., a Chicago department store, was the biggest buyer with an order for 30,000, which it gave away as premiums with the purchase of major appliances. *Best of Football Follies* (NFL) is expected to sell hundreds of thousands of copies when it will also be used as a premium. Consequently, producers can make a profit by selling videos outside the traditional video outlets.

Public Domain

Public domain is not really a genre but should be discussed here just the same. Public domain consists primarily of old feature films and television programs whose copyright owners failed to renew their copyrights; hence, these properties have slipped into the *"public domain."* Public domain material may be duplicated and sold by anyone. No license is necessary. Much of this material was snapped up by Kartes Video (225 titles) and other distributors and sold at low prices (some as low as $9.95) to the bookstore trade. Initially this venture was very successful because it was some of the first sale-only product available. Sales started dropping when consumers realized that the quality of these tapes was often very poor; sound would drop out, picture would drop out, scenes would have scratches or tape splices, etc. In the beginning Kartes' business was 85% public domain. After gaining a customer base, Kartes expanded by distributing a syndicated workshop series, *Wally's Workshop,* and a cooking series. Now public domain titles are only about half of its business and falling fast.

After Kartes' initial success, other manufacturers jumped on the bandwagon and dumped poor-quality product into the marketplace hoping for similar results. Some sold as low as $4. Unfortunately the public was turned off and many merchandisers no longer carry public domain product.

Travel

Travel tapes offer prospective travelers glimpses of places they may wish to visit either in person or in their armchair. What better way to see, hear and gain a sense of where you may be headed? Some airlines, tourist bureaus and travel agencies offer tapes to their clients at no charge. These tapes are often produced by tourist bureaus and sent free to travel agents. Air France has a cassette lending library as does the New Zealand tourist office. Video Brochures International has set up a network of 2,000 travel agencies that make promotional videos available.

Travelvision is a 30-tape series of 45-minute programs at $39.95. Editorially, the series features hotels and restaurants in short commercials within the tape. Travelvision tapes cover such places as Acapulco, Amsterdam, Banff/Lake Louise, Cairo, the Bahamas, British Virgin Islands, Freeport, Guatemala, Jamaica, Lisbon, Nassau, Puerto Vallarta, St. Thomas and St. John.

The *S. Janssen* series of 20-minute tapes explores China, Moscow and the Himalayas at $39.95. The GLL-TV 15-tape series of 60-minute tapes includes *Christmas Around the World* and *Journey to Adventure* at $39. Modern Video has a 60-minute tape series on *Corpus Christi, Hong Kong, St. Moritz, Maui, New England, Luray Caverns Virginia, North Carolina, San Diego* and *Delta Queen*. These tapes are sold at $12 each.

Republic Pictures Home Video has also released tapes on cities such as Los Angeles and New York at $24.95.

Vestron Video is releasing a series of *Rand McNally Video Trips* featuring well-known hosts such as *Annette Funicello's South Florida, Tony Randall's New York,* and *Jill St. John's San Francisco* among others at $29.95.

Other producers/distributors that have entered the genre are Independent United Distributors, *Surprising Europe;* Travelvision International, *Paradise Island* and *Nassau*; West Coast Video Productions, *Feel Hawaii*; Norman Beerger Productions, *Adventures of Kauai*; Travel Video International, *How to Visit Hawaii Local Style*; Environmental Video Inc., *Hawaii Experience*; Videotakes, Inc., *Sunsport Vacations for Winter*; Sallyforth Video, *Stan Delaphan's World of Cruise Ships*; Cityscape Productions, *Nashville*; Wilderness Video, *Yosemite Park* and many others.

While travelers cannot take the tapes with them, as they can a book, these tapes offer an excellent way to prepare for trips or re-enjoy vacations months later. The tapes are sold through video stores, bookstores, travel agencies, airline and souvenir shops and through direct marketing.

Travel tapes are a difficult genre to enter because production expenses are high. Innovative producers will find sponsors such as hotels, tourist bureaus and airlines who may be eager to lend a hand to promote their particular city or country. High-paid celebrity hosts add interest for the consumer and retailer. Credible travel names like Michelin, Fromhers, Fodor or Rand McNally add trusted value.

Many distributors hope to sell their tapes to the travel agencies. However, travel agencies are some of the worst marketers of any retail business. Many feel that the tapes compete with the services they offer; others don't want to set up video players and monitors. Others are reluctant to buy tapes when they can get some free from tourist bureaus. Some retailers argue that a second drawback is that travelers may want to see them only once, making them difficult to sell to own. Nevertheless, the playing field is cluttered with many producers and distributors hoping this will be the next hot genre. By all accounts, it's too early to tell. Many marketing obstacles still have to be overcome.

Specialty

New forms of programming come along all the time. For example, *Cardsettes* are video greeting cards for birthdays, congratulations, Christmas and anniversaries. They sell for $14.95.

Audubon Guide to North American Birds is a reference tape sold by Mastervision for $74.95.

A railroading series is sold by Kalmbach Video on everything you would ever want to know about trains, which must be a lot because there are 44 tapes available.

Astrology Star Signs, 12 cassettes, one for each sign of the zodiac, is available from MCA.

Cooking

In bookstores, cookbooks are a very successful genre. Bookstore cookbook sections have dozens of titles. One would think the equivalent should hold true for cooking videos. As yet, this is not the case. They have not sold well. Why? Perhaps, because they are not easy to use. Most VCRs are in the living room, not the kitchen. How do you use a cooking tape? Do you bring the VCR, monitor and cords into the kitchen? Do you carry your bowls, mixing spoons and ingredients into the living room? It's a clumsy situation at best. Well-designed cooking tapes teach technique. Recipe cards are packaged with the tape. This way you learn what is meant by a *''pinch.''* You study the technique you will use later. The recipe card is used for reference when you cook. In the future, when VCRs have built-in screens and are truly portable, cooking tapes may come of age. Until then, it may continue to be a weak genre.

Here are some examples of cooking tapes that have been released:

The Way to Cook by Julia Child	$29.95	Random House
Yes You Can Microwave	29.95	JCI Video
New Orleans School of Cooking Workout Program	39.95	Creative Video Prod.
Bocuse A La Carte	9.95	Kartes Video
A Guide to Italian Cooking	49.95	Videocrafts Classics
A Guide to Tex-Mex Cooking	49.95	Videocraft Classics
Pasta: Beyond Primavera from Metropolitan Home Magazine	29.95	Video Menus Inc.

WEIGHT WATCHERS®
MAGAZINE
Guide To Dining & Cooking
Hosted By
Lynn Redgrave
Executive Producer Lawrence Kasanoff

Weight Watchers Guide to a Healthy Life Style	29.95	Vestron Video
Weight Watchers Guide to Dining	29.95	Vestron Video
Short-Order Gourmet	29.95	Esquire Video
A Guide to Chinese Cooking	49.95	Videocraft Classics
Craig Claiborne's New York Times Video Cookbook	29.95	Warner Home Video

Sponsored

Sponsored tapes are not a genre but are a new opportunity for producers looking to finance specialized programs. Sponsored tapes are those financed by corporate sponsors. Sponsored tapes can come about in a variety of ways. An advertiser or corporation may finance the production. It may underwrite the marketing effort for a program. Or, the sponsor may buy thousands of completed tapes to give away or resell. Since the producer cannot count on sales through the traditional channels, a sponsor's financing or partial financing often allows the program to be made. Obviously, a sponsor gets involved because the program perpetuates corporate image, allows a product or service to be merchandised, or generates a profit. Tapes are usually not sponsored by corporations for philanthropic reasons.

For example, *Jan Stephenson's Playing A 'Round* is a sponsored golf tape. The producers found three sponsors that were willing to buy back thousands of tapes, at less than wholesale, but more than cost. These sales alone covered the production cost. One sponsor—a golf bag manufacturer—gave the tape away as a sales incentive. When a golfer bought a $500 bag, he got a free tape. Everyone was happy. The sponsors got their names imprinted on the cassette box and on the beginning of the program. They had a specially designed program with their name on it that showed their product. The three sponsors paid for the production before it was shot. The producer didn't have to wait for distribution to cover the costs. His profits came through additional sales in sports stores, pro shops, direct mail and through normal home video distribution.

Karl-Lorimar's tape *Eat to Win* was sponsored by Red Lobster and was one of the first sponsored tapes to receive the attention of the video trade. Although 30,000 tapes were shipped, only about 7,000 to 15,000 units sold. Initially, Karl gave exclusive distribution rights to Ingram, one of its wholesalers, to sell to bookstores first, before releasing the program to the video trade. This may have contributed to low sales when the tape finally entered the traditional video market. Reportedly the program cost $250,000 with an equal amount spent on promotion and advertising.

Magazines can also sponsor tapes. Vestron released a *National Geographic Video* line. The magazine's name prominently appears on the cassette package. The program is sold through direct mail to National Geographic members, through space advertising in the magazine as well as the traditional video outlets. In addition, TDK, the tape stock manufacturer, paid for some consumer advertising and provided the raw tape stock for the program's duplication.

Lightning Video's release of *Rand-McNally's Video Trips* had marketing support and cooperation from Rand-McNally, a leading travel name. Besides the credibility lent by the name, the programs also feature celebrity hosts. The combination of recognizable names immediately raises it above competing travel tapes.

Karl-Lorimar too has entered into co-sponsor arrangements with popular magazines, such as *Consumer Reports*. Here, the magazine's editorial expertise was used to develop the program. When it was finished, the program was advertised through space ads to a very targeted audience.

Serendipity worked out an arrangement with sponsors to participate in Esquire's Success Series. Kodak, contributed tape stock and advertising. Vidal Sassoon's products were featured. *Esquire's Success Series* was aimed at upscale male professionals. The 6-tape series included *Career Strategies I, Career Strategies II, Short Order Gourmet, Persuasive Speaking, Professional Styles* and *The Wine Advisor*. They were projected to sell 50,000 to 100,000 copies each but sold far less. Advertising allotments were reported to be about $500,000 including direct response through Esquire and other magazines. Return policies and profit margins were liberal in order to get the tapes into the distribution channels.

Karl-Lorimar distributed the *Mr. Boston Official Video Bartenders Guide*. (The book sold 10 million copies.) The video sold 5,000 to 10,000 units when it was released. The promotional effort was aimed at bars, liquor stores and buyers of the book. It was priced at $14.95, or $19.95 with the book, or $24.95 with shot glasses.

Producers need to develop programs and sponsor relationships at the same time. It is not worth the effort to develop a program only to find that no sponsors are interested. Producers can begin by talking to sponsor's ad agencies and corporations simultaneously to identify worthwhile programs. Sometimes sponsors will not be interested until they see a finished product. Sometimes corporate dollars are committed years in advance so these sponsored projects need a long lead time.

Also pitching the program's content may be the least effective approach. Sponsors have their own agendas of why they will sponsor a specific program. Corporate image and marketing strategies may have more to do with sponsorship than what the program is about.

At this early stage in home video, it is difficult to sell a potential sponsor and/or advertising agency on the value of a sponsored home video. If they evaluate the program's effectiveness in traditional terms (cost per thousand), they will quickly realize that is far more cost effective to spend their money on newspaper or television advertising. Tapes do not reach many people.

For example, an *"A"* title may sell 100,000 units. Assuming that the tape is rented 100 times (in its life) and seen by two people per viewing, then 20 million impressions occurred. If a sponsor pays $100,000 for production, then it costs $5 for every five thousand impressions. It's far cheaper to use other forms of media.

A specialized title may sell 20,000 units. Making the same assumptions, if the sponsor paid $50,000 toward production, it costs $12.50 per thousand impressions.

Obviously, other benefits must be stressed to entice sponsors. First, if the program is priced low, then it is possible to sell more tapes. But since people will own them, fewer people in aggregate will view each tape compared to tapes from the rental pool. If the program demonstrates how a sponsor's product can be used, this may interest sponsors. A sponsor's profit participation in the program may be an enticement. Producers will need to run a variety of mathematical models to determine a program's benefit to a sponsor. Obviously, whether the tape is intended for rental, or sell-through, or both will affect the numbers.

While there have not been any smash success stories in the sponsored area as yet, there is every indication that as VCR penetration grows, the sponsored community and home video will form an alliance. Much like cable television, new forms take a long time before being absorbed by the sponsored community. Video is still in an embryonic stage.

Producers should begin to form alliances now. Sponsored videos could become a major business and source of video financing in the next five years.

Summary

These are just some of the original program genres that have been successful (or not so successful) to date. More forms will be developed and produced as innovative producers seek out new market channels. Many will fail; some will be super-hits. The best chance producers have is to first grasp what has been done in the past, to understand the marketplace as it exists today and to seek out new market niches and channels of distribution. Every programming opportunity is a marketing opportunity as well.

SUCCESSFUL VIDEO PROGRAMS

Successful Video Programs

"If your idea is hot, distributors will be falling all over each other to take you to lunch."

Successful Video Programs

When a producer decides to make a specific program, that's a programming decision. It is also a marketing decision, because, hopefully, inherent in the project are the seeds for a marketing and promotion campaign. The more a producer thinks about this when designing his program, the more successful the program will be.

Concurrently, when a distributor acquires a program, he is also making a programming and marketing decision. His innermost thought: *"How can this be sold?"*

In 1985, Vestron's original program department reviewed thousands of projects. (The feature, children's and music video departments also evaluated thousands of submissions.) Most failed to combine the necessary elements that would make marketing successful and were rejected.

What are the elements common to best-selling programs that have contributed to their success?

Pre-Exposure

Perhaps the title or subject has already had previous exposure theatrically, on television, in the newspapers, in bookstores, or in music. It's conceivable that there already may be considerable public awareness of the title of the program, its star, or its subject. This represents time and money that a distributor does not have to spend because the subject and title have already been publicized. It is certainly easier to market a program once the tracks have been greased. The program's attraction to the distributor, wholesaler and retailer will be greatly enhanced.

Movies have had multi-million dollar ad campaigns before they hit the video market. The public already has some awareness about the movie, even if some didn't see it. This increases any movie's home video potential. An original program can benefit by pre-exposure as well.

Promotability

The *hook* or promotable element in the project must be easily identified. It must jump out at wholesaler, retailer and consumer alike. Each should readily exclaim, *"aha!"* or *"of course!"* It should be that obvious. The program's hook must instantly grab attention. Remember, it must compete with 500 other titles upon its release. (Sometimes a program is only sold by its title with no accompanying poster, copy lines, or packaging.) Give a program a boost with a strong title, recognizable stars, a clever hook in the sales copy, a terrific package, or hot concept.

Get the star of the tape or host to promote the program on television and radio. A sponsor's involvement in the program may increase advertising and promotional opportunities.

Since a distributor will need to spend considerable money on advertising, promotion and publicity, a pre-promoted project will be very desirable.

If the program idea and packaging is really hot, distributors will be falling all over each other to take you to lunch. If they don't, it probably isn't as hot as you think.

Celebrity Participation

Exercise tapes are everywhere. Those with celebrities, regardless of how well they do the exercises, will get the attention of the trade before their counterparts. Message? Use celebrities. Remember, home video is a movie-driven business. People know movie stars. (Even if the person isn't real—for example, a licensed toy character like Rainbow Brite will bring valuable recognition to the program.)

High Concept Title

"High concept" is a concept that no one in Hollywood really understands but uses all the time when touting a project. *"It's really high concept."* What it means is that the title or the premise of the program is flashy, sexy, or *"gettable"* enough to gain instant recognition. (Now it's perfectly clear, right?)

Truly Tasteless Jokes, Ghost Stories, Private Fantasies, Groove Tube, Sleazamania, Jazzercize, Eroticize, Prime Cuts, Lords of the Ring, Art or Bust, From Mao to Mozart, Women Tell the Dirtiest Jokes, and *Your Erroneous Zones* are all high concept original program titles. High concept isn't necessarily highbrow!

From the title, you get an instant image of what the show is about and how it's presented. Your expectations are then fulfilled by watching the program. Titles should be brief and very descriptive. They should be highly suggestive and pack a wallop. With terrific packaging, the impression can be made even more powerful.

Recognizable Genre

To reiterate. The program itself should fall into a clearly defined genre. Is it a documentary, a comedy, music video or a how-to? Hybrid mixtures of genres will only lead to buyer confusion. There should be no doubt in the producer's mind as to what he's making and no doubt in the buyer's mind as to what he's getting.

Credibility

Lastly, the program itself needs substance, credibility. It needs to be good—to deliver on the marketing hook. *Walter Chronkite, Jane Fonda, National Geographic, ABC News* and *Consumer Report* are all names that are credible. An authority, expert, or established trademark gives viewers confidence that they are getting the real McCoy.

When producers make good programs and keep in mind what elements have made for successful programs in the past, they will increase their chances for a hit. It's a long, laborious process and yet a business and an art that holds much satisfaction. There's many a possible pitfall, and plenty of hard work to be done. At the same time, there are also many of tomorrow's hits waiting to be made. May some of them be yours.

PRE-PRODUCTION

Pre-production

"It's a hot idea . . . how do you begin?"

Pre-production

Let's assume that you've found a subject worthy of production. It's a hot idea, can be readily marketed and you're set to begin. With your kernel of an idea, scratched on the back of a matchbook in a moment of profound inspiration, how do you begin?

Finding a Writer

The idea may be hot but it needs to be massaged into the visual medium of film or video. There are experienced writers who can conform the idea into a format for film and video. Script writing is entirely different than print writing. The final script will approximate a blueprint for production—with camera angles, lighting, dialogue and stage directions. The best way to select a writer is to watch films or videotapes that are similar in genre to your project and then seek out the writer.

If you are doing an instructional tape, examine other instructional tapes. The opening and closing credits will tell you who worked on the production. To find the writer, call the program distributor and ask for the producer's phone number. Or call the producer and ask how you can locate the writer. This method takes you directly to the kind of writer best suited for the tape you want to create.

It also helps to talk to other producers and get their recommendations. Call the Writer's Guild of America (WGA) in Los Angeles and New

York. Buy the directories. Look at local production directories that list writers (and producers) and their credits. Better still, make use of personal references. After half a dozen phone calls, you'll have honed in on several possibilities.

Treatments

Once you've established the premise for your videotape, it's time to write a treatment. The treatment is not a script but rather a shorter exposition on how you plan to "*treat*" the subject. It is a synopsis, a condensation of the material, sequence after sequence. It usually does not contain all the dialogue but rather a sampling. The camera shots are not written out individually until the script stage. The treatment gives you an opportunity to see how the idea feels and allows the writer to make changes without having to do a major rewrite. When the treatment works you go to script stage.

What the Producer Does

A producer is often the one that oversees the development of the entire project. Sometimes that includes the treatment, but not always. Sometimes a producer is hired once the treatment is finished, and it becomes his or her job to determine how it is to be produced and what it will cost. You can find producers by looking at videotapes or films in the same genre as your project. Track down the producer from the credits and see if he'd like to produce your project.

It's the producer's job to organize the production from script through completion. Producers are paid a fee for doing this, and are occasionally given a small percentage of the profits. (This added motivation could pay off in a better production.) Producers may package the program—that is, put together all the elements: actors, director, camera crew, editing staff, post-production editing and recording, etc. Major agencies in New York and Los Angeles such as William Morris, ICM, or APA also package programs.

Working With Agents

Agencies employ agents whose job is to make things happen—to put together talent (writers, directors, producers and actors) for a specific idea. Once packaged, the program can be sold to a distributor or financing entity. Upon successfully providing these elements, the agent (or agency) receives a fee. This fee is usually 10% of the fee that the actor, writer or talent receives. More and more agencies are making home video deals for their clients.

An agency can also represent producers; however, they are not only looking for one-time projects to package and sell but rather a long-term relationship with producers who can develop and execute a series of successful projects. The agency or agent's job is to make frequent contact with buyers and negotiate the most favorable deals for their clients. The more projects a producer will come up with, the more projects the agency has to package, sell and profit from.

Discuss your needs and agency fees before embarking. An agency can bring clout to a project and leverage elements you may not be able to muster on your own. A strong producer can also do this and save a packaging fee. The hotter the idea, the quicker it will come together.

Contact Distributors

If you are looking for producers or directors, distributors can also suggest experienced people. The program development or acquisition department in a distribution company has first-hand experience with a wide variety of talent and may offer ideas. Since someday they will distribute your tape, they may be willing to help you with packaging suggestions.

Once your program is written and packaged with cast and production talent, you are ready to pitch the project for financing and distribution.

FINANCING

Financing

''Every partner brings something to the table, puts something at risk and shares in the upside of the project.''

Video Distributors

If your project is commercial and is a made-for-home project then the best approach for financing might be to contact a video distributor in your search for funds. The upside is that you will find financing and a distributor and can get back to the task at hand—producing. The downside is that whenever you put someone else's money at risk, you will never strike as good a deal as if you had used your own resources.

Like any lending institution the distributor may charge interest on the production funds until it is repaid. Royalties may be smaller since you need financing and are not risking any of your own capital. (You'll almost always get a larger royalty on a completed project.) Any monies advanced from production will be treated like an advance and recouped from gross receipts. Once the investment is recouped, then the producer may participate in profits. Furthermore, since distributors (as investors) are at risk, more than likely they will want some ownership in the other rights in the program to protect their downside. On the other hand, not having to pound the pavement for investors may make a distributor financing arrangement look terrific.

A major benefit in getting financing from a distributor is that you'll never have to worry about whether distributors will work hard for your project. They will. Especially when their money is involved. Self-interest is a tremendous motivator.

Distributors may provide *"interim financing"* whereby they pay out money at various phases of production—upon signing the agreement, approving script, talent and production techniques, commencement of principal photography, approval of an off-line edit or rough cut, and finally, the balance, when the videotape master, and other materials (script, E&O insurance, M&E sound tracks, trailer, color stills, copyright form, etc.) are delivered.

Distributors may also provide a signed contract stating that they will pay X amount of dollars upon receipt of a one-inch master. This is generally referred to as a *"negative pickup."* This binding contract is *"bankable."* You can take it to a bank and obtain a production loan. Interest will be charged until the program is finished and the distributor makes good on the contract.

Another mode is when a distributor simply agrees to pay monies upon delivery of a master, and the producer finances the program through a limited partnership. Or the producer may use deferment financing (he agrees to pay his bills to actors, crew, lab, etc.) when he receives money from the distributor.

There are a variety of ways to work with the distributor in financing your program. Structuring is not that difficult. The real key is designing a program that the distributor values. The better the project, the better deal you can strike.

Limited Partnerships

A limited partnership is a legal instrument whereby funds may be raised from private investors. It is one of the simplest legal forms for financing productions, and is familiar to virtually every lawyer. A good entertainment lawyer has dozens of *"boilerplate"* limited partnership forms on his word processor and can design one for your needs.

The concept is simple. Investors put up money for a share of the partnership's profits. The investors are called limited partners because their liability is limited only to the money they initially invest. They are not liable for overbudget expenses or to commit any additional monies. They are also limited from the day-to-day managing of the partnership's business (in this case, producing a program).

The general partner (usually the producer) is responsible for managing the business of the partnership while it exists, keeping accurate records, and providing tax reports at the end of each year to investors. He or she is also responsible for any over-budget expenses by loaning his or her own money or obtaining a loan to complete production. The general partner is the most vulnerable and liable partner should difficulties arise during production.

In exchange for managing the partnership and acting as producer, the general partner may receive 50% of the profits once the initial investment is paid back to the limited partners. The limited partners as a group receive 50%.

For example, if the production costs $100,000, and $200,000 is returned to the partnership from distribution royalties, then $100,000 is paid back to the investors. If the program fails to repay the initial investment, then the investors take a loss. The general partner is not legally liable or required to pay back the investment if the royalties from distribution fall short. That's the risk all film and video investors share.

Consult a lawyer who can best design a limited partnership following the rules and regulations in the state where you intend to raise your financing. Often the number of investors that you can ask to join the partnership is limited. You can have a limited partnership with one investor or as many as 12 or more, depending on the state where the partnership is filed.

To give greater investment incentives to the limited partners (investors), the split of profits after the investment is repaid is sometimes 60-40 favoring the investors. Another incentive is to repay more than 100% of the original investment (such as 125% or 150%) before the profits are shared with the general partner. The general partner may or may not have invested money in the production in any of these examples.

Many lawyers already have their own *''boilerplate''* forms for limited partnerships, which they can adapt to your specific project. The limited partnership agreement defines how the business will be managed, what controls there are, and how the business will be conducted. It describes the responsibilities of the general partner and states what method will be used to return the investment to the investors. It describes investment tax credit and other issues of concern to the investor. It is a good idea to have both your lawyer and your accountant consult with one another in designing the limited partnerships agreement.

The document should be prepared before you begin raising money. If you find investors, you will want to have the agreement ready to sign rather than waiting the weeks or months it may take to put one together. Investors will have their own lawyers and accountants read the limited partnership agreement before they invest. Being prepared will not give investors time to change their minds.

Make it clear to investors that films or videos are tremendously risky and that they could lose all their money. There are many reasons for this: The project may never be finished, it may never find distribution, it may fail in distribution, or a multitude of other unforeseen problems. When discussing your program with investors, be very conservative when projecting profits, so that expectations are not raised beyond reality. If your project does not have commercial possibilities, and it is unlikely that the project will repay its investors, then it is best to seek alternative financing.

Co-Production Opportunities

Co-productions or joint ventures are another common form used to finance productions. Here, the risk is spread out among any number of direct and indirect users or participants in the project. Any combination of the following could make up a co-production:

—private investors
—facilities (studios, editing houses, recording studios)
—laboratory (film processing, video duplication)
—sponsors (corporate, products and services)
—distributors (film, video, television)
—pay or basic cable systems
—producers (production houses, animation facilities)
—talent
—agencies
—law firms
—stock footage houses
—equipment rental companies
—music publishers
—record companies
—publishers (books, magazines)
—toy companies (owners of licensed characters)
—marketing companies
—others

Creative producers with good projects should have little trouble finding valuable partners to co-venture or co-produce a project. Every partner brings something to the table, puts something at risk and shares in the potential upside of the project. If it fails, the producer alone doesn't take the big plunge—everyone goes down together.

If the producer has done his homework, created a strong package with the aforementioned elements of success, he stands a good chance. The deals will vary significantly depending on the players. A good entertainment lawyer can put together a deal that works for everyone.

The beauty of co-ventures is that you combine strengths and cover weaknesses. Each partner has control of his or her own area, contributes accordingly and participates in the success of the project. Depending on your partners, you can move fast or slow. If everyone is experienced, the group mind approach to financing and production may be very powerful.

Often a producer will attempt to license the various rights (home video, theatrical, television, etc.) in a program to various markets and produce the program with the accumulated advances derived from selling off the rights. At other times, the producers will raise money, produce the program and then hope to sell the various rights to the highest bidder. In the best of these situations, the producer collects more than the production cost and makes a profit. Or he could receive less than the cost and his investors will lose money. A producer's main goal is to maximize his profit potential and to protect his downside. Co-production partners often help do just that.

Pay TV

Some producers design their programs so that they will have a life on pay television and on home video. Vestron has released several comedy home videos that played on HBO. The producer designed an arrangement so that HBO would have one release window, which was followed shortly thereafter by the home video release. Sometimes the releases are *"day and date,"* meaning they occur at the same time. Sometimes home video will go first, and other times pay TV will go first. It is up to the producer to solve the problem of who goes first. Sometimes there will be an advantage to home video going first (usually when the star is well-known), and other times the home video release can use the pay cable pre-exposure to gain publicity for a program (such as when the star or program is not well-known). Sometimes programs are originated for home video and later are broadcast on a pay TV network. *Father Guido Sarducci Goes To College* originated at Vestron Video and was later redeveloped with Showtime so it would meet the needs of both buyers. The more partners, the more money can be raised for the production.

To design a co-production, a producer must approach the pay television service and home video distributor simultaneously. The program needs to be designed so that it will have value in both marketplaces. Sometimes pay TV will require a one-hour show and home video will require a 70-, 80-, or 90-minute program. It is very important to design a program with both releases in mind.

Foreign TV

Some programs are produced as television specials or series and are later compiled or re-edited for home video use. *The Prince and Princess of Wales: Talking Personally* (Vestron) first was produced for English television and later re-edited for home video. Producers can sometimes look for English or German television for financing in exchange for foreign broadcast rights, thereby retaining home video rights. Obviously, the subject matter must appeal to both buyers. It is the creative producer who can find and exploit the needs of two different program users, thereby maximizing financing available. More often than not, the production cost of programs is so high that it requires two or more partners.

PBS/Local Television Stations

Often a local PBS station, such as KCET, WGBH or WNET, or a large independent commercial television station will produce its own programs. Occasionally these programs will also have value as home videos. The same formula applies: The producer gets a license fee or monies toward production from the local station and retains the home video rights that he or she licenses for an additional fee to a home video distributor. Sometimes the program can be licensed intact to home video; at other times the producer must shoot additional material and re-edit. If a producer can work with both buyers simultaneously, he can most effectively design a program for each.

Syndication

Again, the same principles apply. A producer will go to a syndicator to finance a television series and retain the home video rights in order to compile a program or programs from the series for home video release. This most often occurs with producers of children's Saturday morning animated series, which are later repackaged for home video.

Books

Producers can contact authors and book publishers and design programs that release simultaneously with their books. By doing so, the author or celebrity can develop a home video program at the same time as the book. Development costs can be cut. More important, the book and tape can be released simultaneously and take advantage of cross-marketing opportunities. Two of the most successful examples of this approach were the first Jane Fonda tape and *Raquel: Total Beauty and Fitness* (Thorn/EMI).

Facilities

Production studios and editing houses will often defer payment until a home video program is in release and earning royalties. Facilities deals can help cut the initial budget considerably. The facilities often give the producers down-time (evenings and weekends) in exchange for a deferred payment and a small percentage of profits.

Putting It All Together

Enterprising producers will be very creative in combining all available options for financing. They will combine facilities, pay, foreign and syndicated television releases, celebrity participation, book publishers and home video when designing the financing of their productions. Some even go to sponsors to pay for the cost of production and promotion. *With enough deals, a producer can make a profit before the cameras even roll!*

CONSIDERATIONS

Considerations

"Too often, producers complete their programs without consulting distributors. Then it is too late."

Considerations

Once you're financing and distribution is in place, the videotape begins taking shape. There are a few people you may wish to talk to before filming or taping.

Distributor's Considerations

It is advantageous to consult with a distributor or potential distributor who will have very definite suggestions as to the structure of the videotape, the actors hired, etc. The distributor's input is critical because he or she is closest to the marketplace and knows what elements are needed to increase the program's marketability. (If the distributor is financing any portion of the program, then he or she will certainly require approval of the script, budget, talent, and production techniques employed.)

Listen to these suggestions. Too often, producers complete their programs without consulting distributors. Then it is too late. This is unfortunate because often a suggestion or two from a distributor will make a big difference when it comes to marketing and selling a program. Often these comments will not affect the integrity or content of the program, so producers should not be afraid to listen to distributors.

Sponsor's Considerations

The sponsor, if there is one, will also have special needs. He or she may want a special title card, certain products used or displayed within the program in a specific way, etc. (Sponsors may be involved in selection of a director, host and cast.)

Pay TV Considerations

If a pay TV service is co-financing the production, it will undoubtedly have approval of casting. It will also want a producer and/or director that it can trust to deliver a first class quality program, on time and within budget. Producers who are not on the pay TV *"approved list"* can co-produce with producers who are in order to get their program made.

Once distributors, TV programmers, sponsors (and any other financiers) have made their final comments, a final script can be completed. Until then an accurate budget cannot be calculated. Until there is a final shooting script from which a production board can be developed, it is impossible to complete a detailed budget. The production board details the most economical order in which the program will be shot. A storyboard is then prepared detailing the composition and continuity of each shot—often with the cinematographer's input. The storyboard is the blueprint for the production. Once the basic elements of the production have been set, the principal photography is scheduled, cast and crew assembled. Going in, you need to know what the production will cost. You'll need a detailed budget.

THE BUDGET

The Budget

"Pity the producer who overlooks something and hopes his contingency budget will cover it."

The Budget

Shown is a detailed budget for the exercise program *The Couch Potato Workout*. (The producers are convinced it's the next best seller to follow Jane Fonda.) The figures are not actual production costs, but fall within a realistic range. Actual budgets will, of course, vary, based on the producer's ability to negotiate favorable deals on fees, services and materials. Once the script is finished, the exercise tape takes five days of pre-production. Four days are budgeted for on-location principal photography in Idaho. Post-production (editing, narration and sound mixing) takes one month. This is a non-union production so no overtime, meal penalties, or benefits are included. All crew members are hired on a *"buyout basis"* per day.

EXERCISE VIDEO: "THE COUCH POTATO WORKOUT"
NON-UNION DETAILED BUDGET

5 DAYS PRE-PRODUCTION 58 MINUTES
4 DAYS SHOOT 5:1 SHOOTING RATIO

	QUANTITY		COST	SUBTTL	
A. STORY					
TREATMENT & SCRIPT	1	FEE	3,000	3,000	
					3,000
B. TALENT					
1 PRODUCER	1	FEE	14,000	14,000	
2 DIRECTOR	1	FEE	5,000	5,000	
CONSULTANTS	2	FEE	250	500	
3&4 ON CAMERA TALENT (2)	2	FEES	2,000	4,000	
					23,500

	QUALTITY		COST	SUBTTL	
C. PRODUCTION PERSONNEL					
5 PRODUCTION MANAGER	7	DAYS	250	1,750	
6 ASSOCIATE PRODUCER	7	DAYS	300	2,100	
7 ASSISTANT DIRECTOR	7	DAYS	200	1,400	
8 CAMERAMAN	7	DAYS	350	2,450	
9 VIDEO ENGINEER	5	DAYS	150	750	
10 LIGHTING DIRECTOR	5	DAYS	150	750	
11 GRIP	5	DAYS	80	400	
12 PRODUCTION ASSISTANT	5	DAYS	50	250	
13 STILL PHOTOGRAPHER	4	DAYS	100	400	
					10,250
D. TRAVEL & LOCATION EXPENSES					
AIR FARE/PEOPLE:	11	PEOPLE	375	4,125	
HOTEL (55 DAYS)	55	TTL DAYS	30	1,650	
CREW MEALS (55 DAYS)	165	MEALS	15	2,475	
LOCATION FEES	4	DAYS	100	400	
PETTY CASH	4	DAYS	100	400	
GRATUITIES	4	DAYS	25	100	
EQUIP CARTAGE	1	FLAT	1,000	1,000	
MISC. EXPENSES	1	FLAT	500	500	
CREW MINIBUS	4	DAYS	55	220	
CAR RENTAL	4	DAYS	35	140	
WAGON RENTAL	4	DAYS	45	180	
GAS & TOLLS	4	DAYS	45	180	
					11,370
E. VIDEO AND FIELD EQUIPMENT					
CAMERA & RECORDER	4	DAYS	1,500	6,000	
WALKIE-TALKIES	4	DAYS	125	500	
LIGHTING	4	DAYS	225	900	
GRIP EQUIPMENT	4	DAYS	150	600	
HELICOPTER	1	DAY	300	300	
					8,300
F. VIDEOTAPE STOCK					
1″ VIDEOTAPE	8	ROLLS	100	800	
					800
G. NARRATION RECORDING					
STUDIO	4	HOURS	125	500	
AUDIO STOCK	3	ROLLS	30	90	
					590
H. SOUND & MUSIC					
MUSIC & RIGHTS	1	FLAT FEE	2,000	2,000	
AUDIO STOCK	2	ROLLS	20	40	
					2,040
I. VIDEO MIXING					
MIXING STUDIO	10	HOURS	250	2,500	
AUDIO STOCK	1	ROLLS	60	60	
STRIPPING	2	HOURS	75	150	
RELAY	1	HOURS	75	75	
					2,785

	QUANTITY		COST	SUBTTL	
J. TITLE CARDS					
TITLE DESIGN	1	FEE	500	500	
MAIN TITLE CARDS	7	EACH	75	525	
					1,025
K. VIDEO EDITING					
TRANSFER VIS-CODE DUBS	8	HOURS	120	960	
3/4" VIDEOCASSETTES	8	CASSETTES	21	168	
OFF-LINE EDITING (1 WEEK)	40	HOURS	125	5,000	
1" CMX EDITING (3 DAYS)	32	HOURS	375	12,000	
ADDITIONAL PLAYBACK MACHINE	32	HOURS	75	2,400	
ADO	12	HOURS	250	3,000	
CHYRON	10	HOURS	200	2,000	
VIDEOTAPE STOCK	1	HOUR	110	110	
BASICKING	1	HOUR	75	75	
PROTECTION MASTER	1	HOUR	175	175	
DUBS	5	DUBS	61	305	
					26,193
K. OFFICE					
OFFICE RENT	3	MONTHS	150	450	
TELEPHONE	3	MONTHS	500	1,500	
FREIGHT & SHIPPING	3	MONTHS	300	900	
PHOTOCOPYING	3	MONTHS	50	150	
OFFICE SUPPLIES, MISC.	3	MONTHS	100	300	
LEGAL FEES	1	FEE	3,000	3,000	
E&O INSURANCE	1	FEE	4,500	4,500	
ACCOUNTING FEES	1	FEE	2,000	2,000	
STORAGE FEES	1	YEAR	72	72	
					12,872
SUB-TOTAL				102,725	102,725
PRODUCTION INSURANCE	0.04%	SUBTL	102,725	4,109	4,109
CONTINGENCY	0.15%	BUDGET		16,025	16,025
		TOTAL		$122,859	122,859

The treatment and script cost $3,000 flat. Once the writer completes several drafts, his job is over. (Cheap because since it is mostly exercise, very little dialogue is written.)

The producer receives a flat fee of $14,000; the director, a $5,000 flat fee. Two consultants ($250 each) are hired from the National Couch Potato Association, who make sure the nationally approved spud exercises are performed. Two local TV talk show hosts (not so famous yet) receive $2,000 each for four days of work.

The production personnel are hired for the extent of the shoot. A still photographer ($125 per day x 4) shoots color slides and black and white stills that will be used for packaging and promotion. Everyone but the actors must travel to the Idaho location, so air fare, meals, and location expenses must be expensed. A location fee of $100 per day is required for rental of the potato farm barn that is the primary location. Cars are rented locally. A video camera and recorder package are rented (four days) along with a set of walkie-talkies. *(It's not a real movie unless you use walkie-talkies!)* The production manager or assistant director needs these to keep the production assistants (PAs) busy at all times.

A helicopter adds *"real production value."* Imagine the opening three-minute title sequence—a single shot—an aerial shot of a potato patch at dawn as we pull into a single potato.

Other budgetary items are the videotape stock required for the shoot itself, a studio session for narration recording, and sound mixing when all the sound (dialogue, narration, sound effects and music) is combined. The opening title art card is designed for $500. Individual title art cards are typeset at $75 each.

The director must have authentic polka music ($2,000 license fee) for the exercise sequences. The original camera master videotapes are transferred to 3/4-inch or 1/2-inch cassettes (with *"window dubs"* or *"vis-code"*), which display the time-code numbers at the bottom of the picture for easy identification of each image. When the off-line editing is complete, the editor will have a frame-accurate list of time-code numbers. He takes these numbers to the 1-inch on-line editing session and can quickly (in our case, three days) assemble a master tape, the primary editing decisions having already been made. (Off-line editing is a standard practice in preparing for the very expensive on-line editing.)

Because there is so much material to edit, an additional playback machine is added so that reels do not have to be changed frequently. An

ADO is booked for 12 hours for flashy visual effects and a Chyron (title generator) adds subtitles to each exercise sequence.

The budget includes the videotape stock for the master, basicking (a process that adds a time-code reference track and prepares the videotape stock for editing), a *''protection copy''* (in case something dreadful should happen to the master), and dub copies for the producer, director, sponsor and distributor.

The producer's budget includes overhead expenses: rent, telephone, shipping, freight, photocopying and so on. He'll probably include money for legal fees to clear the music rights and to negotiate the distribution contract. *''E&O''* refers to errors and omissions insurance and is required by the distributor in case someone crawls out of the woodwork and claims to hold rights to some material used in the production. The E&O insurance protects both producer and distributor from being liable for additional payments. Accounting and storage fees are miscellaneous expenses.

Production insurance covers liability during taping, loss, or damage to the original tapes, damage to equipment, injury to cast and crew, etc. It is calculated as a percentage of the budget. (Some E&O insurance comes as part of the total production insurance package.)

A 15% contingency fund is added for unforeseen production expenses, extra days of shooting due to bad weather, overtime, and such. A contingency fund is normally added as a percentage to most budgets depending on the complexity of the shoot.

In large budgeted productions, a completion bond is purchased. This bond protects the financier from over-budget expenses. This bond is not cheap and can cost 5%-10% of the total budget.

Sometimes half of the bond fee is refundable if the production comes in on or under budget. Since this is a low-budget production with a short shooting schedule and relatively few elements that can go wrong, the producers have decided to forgo this expense. If there are over-budget expenses, the producer will pay for them out of his fee.

Everything that is needed for the production is budgeted. Pity the producer that forgets something but hopes his contingency budget will cover it. The producer uses his detailed budget to compare actual expenses when they come in. If he is running over in one area, he may try to cut back in others. At this point, it's up to him to bring the program within budget.

Note: A detailed explanation of a wide variety of budgeting techniques including negotiation and accounting practices is covered in Wiese's ***FILM AND VIDEO BUDGETS*** and is available through the mail order form in the back of this book.

RIGHTS

Rights

"The producer must warrant that he has obtained all rights in the film."

Rights

There are numerous rights that a producer must acquire in order to distribute his program. Some rights are acquired prior to production such as talent and crew agreements, and literary rights. During production, there are photo releases for extras, location permits and releases. After production there may be music rights clearances and stock footage rights.

Once the program is finished, the producer will then copyright his production (which is in essence a bundle of rights) with the *Library of Congress* in Washington, D.C. Copyright forms called *PA* can be obtained from that office, are relatively easy and inexpensive ($10) to submit.

Obviously, in order to re-license his film to a distributor or television programmer, the producer must warrant that he has obtained all rights in the film and provide any necessary backup documents that may be required. Any insurance company will not issue E&O insurance until it has examined all the backing documents. It behooves a producer to make sure that his releases and clearances are written in such a manner as to satisfy the insurance company. Otherwise, he may have to go back and get signatures on insurance company approved forms. An easy way around this is to have the insurance company pre-approve the forms used. It is doubly important to have E&O insurance because most distributors will not accept the program without it.

Licensing Agreements

Here are examples of licensing agreements for talent, stock footage and music. No claim is made here that these forms are acceptable to E&O insurance companies. Producers should consult with their lawyers and insurance company for acceptable forms. These examples are shown for educational purposes only.

Short Form Talent Release Form for Clip Use

Big Shot Film Productions
1010 Money Bags Lane
Beverly Hills, CA

RE: COUCH POTATO WORKOUT

Gentlemen:

I, the undersigned, do hereby consent to the use of excerpts including my name, image, voice and performance from the (film/program) described below in connection with the picture currently entitled COUCH POTATO WORKOUT, and for no other purposes, as it shall be distributed and broadcast in all media throughout the world, in perpetuity.

I hereby acknowledge that you may be utilizing the aforementioned excerpts in such picture, without compensation to me, and that you are acting in reliance upon this release and grant of rights.

This consent will allow you to use my name and likeness in any advertising or publicizing for this film.

Production(s): "This Great Potato Land Of Ours"—
Approx. two minutes (2:00) from the industrial film by Hermann S.A. Lardo

Very truly yours,

Name: Date:
Address:

Stock Footage Release Form

Hot Shot Productions
1010 Money Bags Lane
Beverly Hills, CA

RE: ''This Great Potato Land of Ours''

Gentlemen:

In accordance with your request, we will permit you to use several excerpts from the above named program totalling two minutes (2:00) of footage in the manner prescribed below. In consideration thereof, you agree as follows:

1. You hereby warrant and represent that said footage will be incorporated solely within the film ''The Couch Potato Workout'' and may be distributed in all media in perpetuity on a worldwide basis.

2. Our grant to you for use of the excerpts in the manner provided is strictly conditional on your assumption of all guild, union and other obligations incurred by virtue of you to use of the excerpts and on your obtaining prior written agreements from all appropriate guilds (i.e. AFTRA, AFM, etc.) and other parties acknowledging they will look soley to you and not XYZ Corp. for payment of appropriate reuse and other fees.

3. You understand that our granting of this permission to use footage from above-named picture is on a non-exclusive basis, and that we make no warranties or representations with respect to this grant. You agree to indemnify, defend and hold us harmless against any and all claims, demands, liabilities, loss and/or damage (including reasonable attorney's fees) arising out of, or in connection with, your possession and/or use thereof. You undertake to obtain all other necessary waivers, permissions or approvals and pay all residuals, reuse or other fees payable under any collec-

tive bargaining or other agreement which may be payable because of your use of the excerpt. You further assume all responsibility for all laboratory or other costs which may arise in connection with the use of the footage. Ownership and title to the footage used and all rights in and to the motion picture and all elements thereof shall remain at all times with us and we do not, by giving you this permission, grant or transfer to you any rights other than permission to use the footage in the manner specified above.

4. In consideration of the rights granted above, you agree to pay XYZ Corp. at the rate of $1 per minute, totalling $2 (Two) United States Dollars for use of said footage and to provide the following courtesy credit: Excerpts from ''This Great Potato Land of Ours'' courtesy XYZ Corp.

Kindly confirm your agreement by signing in the space below.

Very truly yours,
XYZ Corp.
By:

Agreed to and Accepted:
HOT SHOT PRODUCTIONS
By:

Synchronization Recording License—
Television (Deal Memo Form)

You, (the ''Producer'' referred to in (A)) have advised us, in our capacity as Agent for our publisher-principal(s), referred to in (C) (herein referred to as ''Publisher''(s)) that you wish to obtain certain rights (herein referred to as the ''License Rights'') to use the musical composition referred to in (B) (herein referred to as the ''Composition'') for the purposes and upon the terms and conditions set forth on the reverse side hereof.

(A) Producer: Big Shot Productions
(B) Composition: Big Polka Tune Writer: Yosh Shmenge
(C) Publisher(s) and Payment Percentage:
Cabbage Rolls and Coffee Music 100%
(D) Picture: The Couch Potato Workout
(E) Territory: World
(F) Period: 5 Years
(G) Use: Type: See Below
(H) License Fee: $2,000
(I) Additional Provisions:

The period in (F) above shall commence from the date of the home video release.

Very truly yours,

Polka Publishers Corp.

By:

Agreed to and Accepted (Producer):

Talent Agreement

As of ______________________________

(date)

Mr./Ms. ____________________________________ (Artist's Name)

(Artist's Address)

Dear ___________________ :

This letter will confirm the agreement reached between XYZ Production Company ("XYZ") and you ("Artist") with respect to Artist rendering personal services as a comedy performer for the show tentatively entitled "A Night of Comedy." ("Program")

1. XYZ hereby engages Artist, and Artist hereby accepts such engagement to provide Artist's services as a performer in connection with the videotaping of the Program. Artist will render her services on or about July 2, 1985. Artist and XYZ will mutually agree on the comedy material to be performed by Artist. Artist shall perform for approximately fifteen to twenty minutes which shall be videotaped with the understanding that all, a portion, or none, of said videotape may be used in the Program.

2. (a) In consideration of Artist rendering such performing services and all other Artist obligations hereunder, XYZ shall pay Artist the sum of ($ amount) dollars at the conclusion of Artist's services on July 2, 1985.

(b) In the event the cost of producing the program is recouped by the financier, XYZ shall be receiving royalties thereafter from the exploitation of the Program in all media. As further consideration, but only in the event any portion of Artist's performance is used in the final edited version of the Program, XYZ shall pay artist (___%) percent of its gross royalties within thirty (30) days of having received said royalties.

3. The Program shall be copyrighted by XYZ, or its assignee, as author, and deemed a "work for hire" owned by XYZ and entirely XYZ's property. Artist hereby grants XYZ the exclusive and perpetual worldwide rights of every kind and nature whatsoever in and to the Program, the results and proceeds of all Artist's services in the Program, the use of Artist's services in the Program, and the use of Artist's material in the Program, on a non-exclusive basis. Such rights shall include, but shall not be limited to, the right to exhibit the Program on television, in theaters, and in any and all other media, including the right to distribute video cassettes, video discs and all other audio-visual devices whether now known or hereafter invented, and by radio broadcast, in audio records, cassettes and tapes, and in books, magazines and other printed material. The foregoing notwithstanding, Artist may perform her entire repertoire of comedy material at live engagements and in all media, except that Artist specifically agrees not to have the material, which is used in the final edited version of the Program, videotaped commercially for a third party for distribution in Home Video and Pay Television markets until after commercial release of video cassettes of the Program, or until six (6) months after the taping of the Program, whichever is sooner.

4. Artist also grants XYZ the perpetual right (but not the obligation), to use Artist's name, voice, photograph, likeness and biography in publications, on jacket covers and other packaging, and for advertising, publicity, promotion and merchandising purposes in connection with the program and all ancillary, subsidiary and derivative rights thereof.

5. On the condition that Artist satisfactorily completes all services required hereunder and Artist appears in the Program released to the general public, then Artist shall be given credit on all positive prints or derivatives of the Program in either the main or end titles, or both.

6. Artist warrants, represents and covenants that the material performed by Artist shall be wholly original (except for material in the public domain or supplied by XYZ) and that the material will not violate or infringe upon

the personal, private or other rights of any person or entity, nor constitute any form of defamation. Artist further warrants, represents and convenants that Artist is free to enter into this agreement and that Artist has not made and will not make any grant or assignment, or do anything which will or might detract from the rights granted to XYZ hereunder.

7. Artist agrees to indemnify XYZ and hold XYZ and all its agents, employees, assignees and licensees safe and harmless from and against any and all liability, loss, damage, cost or expenses, including reasonable attorney's fees, paid or incurred by reason of any breach or default of Artist's covenants, representations and warrȧnties hereunder.

8. If, due to any cause not entirely within XYZ's control, including without limitation, acts of God, accidents, labor controversies, fires, riots or war, XYZ's normal business operations become commercially impractical, then, without limiting XYZ's rights, XYZ shall have the right to suspend operation of this agreement for the period of such force majeure by giving written notice to Artist, and in such event, the current period of the term will be extended for a period equal to the time of such suspension.

9. XYZ, in its sole discretion, may assign this agreement, or the Program produced, or any of XYZ's rights hereunder to any third party. This agreement shall inure to the benefit of and be binding upon the successors, permitted assigns and representatives of the parties hereto. Artist hereby agrees to cooperate to the fullest extent with such third party in connection with the Program produced hereunder, and Artist also agrees to execute such documents as XYZ or such third party may reasonably require in connection with Artist's obligations hereunder, XYZ's obligation to such third party, and Artist's obligation to such third party.

10. This agreement shall be construed pursuant to the laws of the State of California governing contracts fully made to be performed entirely

within California. It is the entire agreement between the parties and may not be modified except by a written instrument signed by both XYZ and Artist. Invalidity or unenforceability of any part of this agreement shall not affect the validity or enforceability of the balance thereof. Waiver of any provisions of this agreement shall not affect XYZ's rights thereafter to enforce such provisions, or to exercise any right or remedy in the event of any other default. Each party hereto must give the other at least thirty (30) days notice of any breach or default hereunder, and the party receiving such notice shall have thirty (30) days from the receipt thereof within which to cure said breach or default.

11. All notices or demands which either party shall be required or desire to give to the other hereunder shall be in writing at the addresses indicated above, or at such other address as a party shall designate in writing, and shall be given by either personal delivery, or delivery by registered or certified mail, return receipt requested.

Kindly acknowledge your agreement and acceptance of the foregoing by signing below where indicated and returning one copy of this agreement to us.

Yours Sincerely,	Agreed to and Accepted:
By____________________	By____________________
President	(Artist's Name)
XYZ Production Company	

Guild Payments

While we are on the subject of rights payments there might also be payments due the unions and guilds. Particularly in the area of original program compilations where preexisting footage is assembled to create a new program, the producer may be responsible for guild payments where a guild was involved in the original creation of the material.

Unfortunately these payments that need to be made to the various guilds could make such a show prohibitive in terms of budget. Once all the guild payments have been made, the show may not have value in the marketplace in relationship to what the show actually cost to assemble. For example, many BBC dramas would make excellent home videos but the costs of clearing one program could be as high as $60,000 or more, depending on number of actors and musicians employed in the original production. A cultural program from the BBC may not sell enough units to recoup the guild payments. A few years ago, the packagers of *Saturday Night Live* ran into this same problem, and rather than assemble the best of sequences (the costs would have been enormous because payments would have had to be made to every actor, musician, writer, and director for each clip), they simply took original shows and packaged them for release, with no editing of material from other shows. Consequently they only had to make a single payment to all the guilds.

Although these figures may vary and change with new guild negotiations the concept will be valuable. For example, to clear one episode from a network television show, which normally is 48 minutes long, the required payments are as follows: (Note: Producer's gross is the royalties monies a producer receives from the home video distributor and not the total gross a distributor receives.)

For *Screen Actor's Guild (SAG),* payments are 3.6% of producer's gross. For an *AFTRA* show produced before 1973, the fee is negotiable. After 1982, the fee is 2% of producer's gross for variety shows and 3.6% for dramatic programs. For all other programs produced after 1983, it is 2% of producer's gross. These percentages go to the actors appearing in the program.

For the *Directors' Guild of America (DGA)*, programs produced between 1971 and 1984 receive 1.2% of the producer's gross and after 1984, 1.5% of the producer's gross, escalating to 1.8% after the producer's gross reaches $1 million.

For the *Writers' Guild of America (WGA),* programs produced from 1971 to 1985 receive 1.2% of producer's gross. Those programs produced after 1985 receive 1.5% of producer's gross. These figures may change as the various guilds renegotiate their contracts, so it is important to contact the guilds directly. (There also continues to be a great deal of confusion over this issue by producers, lawyers and guilds alike, so your research may turn up contradictory information. The path is still frought with problems as this area is still in flux. Payments do not have to be made to both SAG and AFTRA on one show unless one is using material from both theatrical features and television programs in a compilation. The *AFM (American Federation of Musicians)* requires that if the program is shot on tape, the producer must pay 1% of his gross; if it is shot on film, each musician gets $37 on the tape's initial release and another $37 when the distributor's gross equals $62,500. This amount then escalates up depending upon the distributor's gross. The producer should contact the AFM for a better understanding of this somewhat confusing payment schedule.

To shed some light on this, let's try an example. Let's say you wanted to clear a *Bonanza* show clip (hypothetical example only), regardless of the clip length, you might pay:

AFTRA	3.6% of $50,000 (PG) =	$ 1,800
DGA	1.2% of $50,000 (PG) =	600
WGA	1.2% of $50,000 (PG) =	600
AFM	$37 x 20 musicians =	740
Footage Owner	$500/min x 48 =	24,000
Music Publisher $.06 advance		
	3 songs x 10k cassette units =	1,800
	Total	$ 29,540

(Note: Model assumes a producer's gross of $50,000.)

In our hypothetical model the producer shells out nearly $30,000 to clear all the rights in one episode of *Bonanza.* He receives a $50,000 advance against royalties (which is deemed producer's gross). After clearing rights, he has $20,000 left over for legal fees, overhead, mastering, titling and finishing costs, and his own fee, if there's anything left. If he receives any future royalties from distribution he will again have make payment to the guilds.

If the same producer wanted to combine three episodes of Bonanza on one tape, he'd have to pay nearly $90,000 in rights costs. Only a few compilations might be worth a $90,000 advance and Bonanza probably isn't one of them.

In summary, rights clearances will make up a significant part of any compilation program. A producer should research what these costs are likely to be before proceeding. There are still many successful compilations to be made, but many rights holders believe their rights may be more valuable than they are. Without good negotiating skills, a producer had better have some pretty deep pockets.

GETTING IN THE BUSINESS

Getting In The Business

"It is relatively easy to rent studio space, editing and post-production facilities."

Staffing Up

The entire process of financing, producing, marketing and manufacturing videos is complex. Many different skills are required. Fear not, you don't have to master them all. There are hundreds, even thousands of freelancers that can provide every service. There are consultants, producers, directors, production managers, art directors, camera persons, technicians, and editors in every major city. Regional production directories are helpful when making initial contacts. Call your state film council. They often provide local production directories.

It is relatively easy to rent studio space, editing and post-production facilities. For distribution there are hundreds of them, small and large, handling many genres of programming, including entertainment, informational, adults' and children's films, features, exercise, business and health. There is a listing of some of the better-known distributors in the appendix of this book. Study distributors' catalogs for a better understanding of what they carry. Talk to other video producers. Then select the right combination of talent for your production. Because the process of designing, producing and marketing video is so complex (and expensive), the message for anyone thinking about entering the video market would be—determine the kind of programming that you want to produce or acquire. Make sure a market niche exists. Find a consultant or hire an employee with the expertise to either find programming or oversee original program production.

If you need an acquisition person (someone to buy finished programs), look for people in similar businesses like pay TV, TV syndication, publishing, or among non-theatrical distributors. If you need a development person (someone who thinks up and implements original ideas), then look for someone with an inherent sense of good programming, good judgment and an understanding of what is already being distributed. If you intend to produce original programming, a competent, creative producer with a track record might fill the bill.

If you don't intend to distribute your program through existing distributors, you'll need to hire someone with expertise in sales and marketing. Someone who can design and implement a marketing and sales program for your completed productions. Since most such experts are already employed by video distributors, your search will be a difficult one. You can seek out sales and marketing people from similar fields, such as the record industry or publishing. They'll need to understand mass merchandising, promotion, and sales incentive programs; be able to design a marketing plan; and have the personality to sell your product. This is by far the most difficult task, since the video market is already crowded with accomplished players. A better solution is to research the marketplace and distributors, and develop a program or product line that can find a home with an established, powerful distributor.

Production is where the idea actually becomes real. It is no longer an idea, no longer a script, but the combined elements begin to assemble themselves into something tangible—the final product begins to emerge. The skill of the producer comes into play. Will the original notion actually work on film or tape? What follows is a brief explanation of the process in its simplest form. It sounds easier than it is!

The Production

Picking up from where we left off, we move from pre-production (when the program is being designed) to production—the moment of truth. Once the producer or production manager has completed a budget and production schedule, he or she will assemble the crew.

Most producers hire crew they have worked with before—people they know and trust. The fewer surprises, the better the chances for the project to come in on budget.

Talent agencies can help in casting the various roles. They will send their actors to casting sessions until you find the ones you want. You can call more than one agency, maximizing your possibilities for finding the right cast.

If a sound stage is required, the producer will seek out a studio and negotiate rates with the studio manager. Prices will vary depending on where the studio is located, its size, lighting and camera equipment required, set and prop shop accessibility, and other factors.

Post-Production

A producer will suggest post-production and editing facilities. These will probably be places they've worked with in the past, where they know the editors or can strike the best deals. (A good editor who works fast can save significant production dollars.) Since studios and editing facilities have a tremendous investment in their capital equipment, a producer may negotiate favorable rates by working at night or on weekends, when their equipment is not normally in use. They may also defer payment in exchange for a small share of the tape profits. The producer's ability to negotiate favorable deals will be influenced by how hungry the production facility is for new business.

On-line editing, which uses computerized systems and sophisticated 1-inch recorders, can cost from $300 to $600 or more per hour. This is obviously not the kind of environment where you sit around being creative. It's too expensive to experiment. Consequently, most editing decisions are made during the off-line session and conformed later during on-line editing. Off-line editing is a cheaper, scaled down editing process that is done prior to on-line editing (which is necessary for finishing a videotape master). Off-line rates range from $75-$150 per hour.

The major "creative" decisions occur during the off-line session, when the editor can devote his attention to visual effects, titling, and other post-production aspects. Although this description is an oversimplification of the editing process, it does stress the importance of being prepared before the on-line session begins. The savings will be enormous if care and planning are taken.

Many editing houses or post-production facilities have computer graphics and animation capacities for show openings, title sequences, and special visual effects. These are particularly useful for illustrating things that are difficult for the camera to see (like the inside of the human body). Computer graphics are also useful for displaying graphs, maps, and other art material.

Narration is taped in a few hours in a recording studio. This will be added during either the on-line editing or the video sound mixing session, along with the music.

Original music can be composed and recorded or it can also be licensed from a music library for a minimal charge. (Recording original music is far more costly. Composers, copyists, musicians, recording studios, and mixing facilities all must be hired.) Sound effects can be recorded during the shoot, or bought from a sound effects library. All sound elements—voices, narration, music and sound effects—are mixed together in a sound mixing or sound "*sweetening*" session, as it is sometimes called.

Once the picture has been edited and the sound elements mixed, the final sound track is "*layed onto*" the video master. For safety a second *"protection copy"* is made. A third video master is made for duplicating cassettes en masse.

At this point the producer delivers the master video tape to the client or manufacturer/distributor, who packages and manufactures the cassettes in various formats (VHS, Beta, 8mm, videodisc). The distributor designs preview trailers, posters, point-of-purchase (POP) displays, and other marketing tools in an effort to sell the cassettes to wholesalers, retailers, and consumers.

DISTRIBUTION

Distribution

"Producers are the first to overestimate the sales potential of their projects."

Distribution

Producers who need security will come up with a terrific idea and strike a distribution deal with a distributor before going into production. The deal will either provide that the distributor finance the program or pay for the program when it is delivered. This way, the producer will not be scurrying to make a distribution deal when the program is finished. He or she will know that the hard work during production will pay off and the program will actually be distributed. Other producers, confident that they've got the next *Thriller, Fonda,* or *Chicago Bears Shuffle* will produce their program and then go looking for a distributor. Either way, at one time or another, you'll have to find one to work with.

Finding distributors is not as difficult as it may seem. In the back of the book, there is a list of distributors.

Distributors do differ in terms of the kind of product they distribute, the kinds of deals that can be struck, and in other ways. It behooves the producer to study video distributors' catalogs and business practices prior to even contacting them. The producer should do some market research first and learn what markets the distributors sell to. Do they sell to video retail stores, bookstores, mass merchandisers, toy stores, convenience stores and/or other specialty outlets? How do they distribute? Do they distribute direct, through wholesalers, or through direct mail? How are their products priced—high, low? What kind of marketing campaigns have been designed for original programs in the past? Which ones stand out and which ones look the best? What market share does the distributor have? Is it a big or a small distributor? Do they have the clout or the experience to successfully market your original program? What similar product do they distribute, and how successful was it? If all these questions are answered favorably, then you may have found your distributor.

On the business side, what kind of advance do they offer? How long will it take to recoup the advance before the producer begins sharing overages? How many years will the distributor want an exclusive license? What royalty percentage will be given? Is the royalty based on gross receipts or net receipts?

Regarding marketing and promotion: Will a special campaign be designed for your original program? Will there be a poster? Will there be a one-sheet? Will there be other marketing tools designed to help gain attention for your program in the marketplace? Will trade ads be placed? Where? How will consumers be made aware of the program? Through print ads, radio, TV or via other methods? Will the program be sold through direct response? How many of these ways will the distributor attempt to market your program? Has the distributor used these techniques to market and sell any other programs?

These and other questions should be explored. You should be able to narrow your list of distributors down to three and then rate them in terms of who you think will do the best job based on your own market research. Feel free to contact other producers whose product is distributed by your potential video distributor, and ask them about the satisfaction they have received. Ask how their film was promoted, what kind of advance they received, what their sales figures were, and any other pertinent information that you can obtain.

More than anything, this will help you to determine exactly how valuable your program is in the marketplace, and also allow you to project some realistic—not inflated—sales goals. (Producers are the first to overestimate the sales potential of their projects.)

If you have not yet produced a program, then you must take another approach with distributors. Since you don't have a finished piece of work to show, you must get a distributor to fall in love with your idea, and hopefully, finance it.

Presenting Your Ideas

Distributors are busy people. Ever since the home video market exploded, producers of every kind of program imaginable have come out of the woodwork. Distributors' phones are ringing off the hook. (It is not uncommon for me to receive 80 phone calls a day from producers with project ideas.) Your call will be one more in this video gold rush. How can you make yours stand out? How can you get the attention you need?

Hopefully you will have something that a distributor will want. If you understand the marketplace and how things are sold, you can begin to get into the distributor's head to see what kind of product he is trying to acquire. Present your program with its best foot forward. The program should be highly commercial, easy to promote. It should be made up of some of the elements we have already discussed that make for a successful program, such as strong title, celebrity participation, hot topic, repeatability, and so on. In short, the distributor/financier should "*get*" and love your program from your first sentence. If you have to explain it, you're dead.

If your program is already completed, then it's a relatively simple matter of sending your videotape to the distributor for evaluation. Make sure you have labeled the cassette, and if possible, enclose it in a mock-up of the cassette jacket—this will make your program stand out when it is on the distributor's desk. Often an acquisition department will have your cassette for many weeks or even months, and if it is well packaged, it may pique the evaluator's interest and he or she will screen it before the others. An accompanying letter should briefly describe the program. Do not send 10,000 reviews and letters from people who loved the show. A simple synopsis and a few stills that can be used on the packaging should be more than enough for you to get a response from a distributor.

If your program is only half completed, that is, if you only have some of the program shot or packaged, it is best to speak to the distributor so that if need be you can add elements that may make the tape more marketable. If it is half completed, you must know what you need in terms of financing for completion. If the program is simply an idea, it's best to write it down briefly, describing the major promotable elements. If the distributor is interested in your program based on a one-page outline, he may then request a treatment or a script. It is not necessary to send all materials at once. In fact, it may be better to wait to see what kind of interest you get.

All of these submissions can be followed up with phone calls. Do not make a nuisance of yourself. It will only negatively affect interest in working with you. On the other hand, don't expect to send something in the mail and necessarily get a quick answer. It doesn't hurt to contact the program development or acquisition person at regular intervals to see how the evaluation of your program is coming. Be prepared to provide any information that will help interest them in taking on your program. In the long run, however, their decision will be made on how valuable they think your program is in the marketplace.

They will evaluate your program with one thing on their minds: How many copies will it sell? They'll wonder at what price it can be sold, is it a renter or a sell-through program, can it be sold internationally, can it be marketed through alternative distribution channels? How much effort will it take to make it successful?

The Presentation

Send color stills or artwork. Send a very brief synopsis. It should be well-written, snappy, and highlight the promotable elements. (If you want to understand what they are looking for, go to any video store and read the back of any videocassette package.) If you can afford it, edit a one-minute trailer or put together a highlights reel. By submitting your program in this form, a distributor can review the material in less than five minutes and not miss any of the highlights that make your program marketable. Moreover, you've gone right to the point, helped them with their job and not wasted their time. Believe me, this will be much appreciated.

Once you've gained their interest, of course, they will want to see the entire program and any supporting materials you may have. (Now is the time to send your 10,000 reviews—or actually the best ones for the package and poster.)

If you haven't completed the program, the distributor will want to see a detailed budget, a script, cast list, and shooting schedule. These can be sent once you have piqued their initial interest with your other materials.

Few people realize how little they need to get the attention of a distributor. For some reason producers think that more is better. But when you are a development or acquisitions person receiving literally hundreds of programs a month, *"short and sweet"* will be greatly appreciated and you will get a short and sweet response, hopefully a *"yes, let's do it."*

You should also have an idea of what kind of deal you are looking for. That is, how much money you want for production or as an advance, a realistic understanding of royalties and so forth. You won't get too far by being coy and asking, *"Well, how much will you pay for this?"* Ask for what you want.

If you have completed your program, a distributor will want to see your E&O insurance, backing release documents for talent and music, and hear any ideas you may have for marketing it—particularly if it is a specialized project. Perhaps you can acquire a mailing list or free promotional ads in a specialized magazine. Tell the distributor your ideas and any contacts you have that will be useful.

The distributor will be pleased if the celebrity that appears in your tape is willing to help promote it. If this is the case, be sure to bring it to the distributor's attention. It will be of considerable value and increase your odds for a more favorable deal, as it helps the distributor market the tape.

So, the distributor loves your idea. It's everything he hoped for in a presentation. Now what?

MAKING THE DEAL

Making The Deal

''Spend a few hours educating yourself now rather than finding out later you made a poor deal.''

Making the Deal

Before negotiating a home video deal, producers should do their homework by gathering a basic understanding of contracts so that when they begin a distribution deal, they will be better prepared. Contract terms and delivery requirements may vary from distributor to distributor. It's better to spend a few hours educating yourself now rather than finding out later that you made a poor deal. Only when you realistically understand what revenues will flow to you from distribution can you make useful income projections. Take your time during this part of the process as it will be something you'll have to live with for the length of the contract.

What follows are some explanations and definitions of terms found in most contracts. Consult your lawyer for a more thorough understanding. This is only meant to give basic information and should in no way be considered legal advice.

Exclusive Rights

Any home video distributor you select will have the exclusive rights to the program. That is, the distributor will have the sole rights to manufacture and distribute your program. You cannot make deals with other distributors until the distribution agreement has expired.

Distribution Markets

Since there are a variety of markets available to a distributor, which include video retail outlets, mass merchandisers, bookstores, toy stores, convenience stores, direct marketing and others, a distributor will want to maximize potential revenues by distributing in all these markets. On a rare occasion it may be possible to split off some of these rights. For example, if a distributor decides not to sell your cassette through direct mail, you may be able to reserve these rights and handle direct mail yourself or license these rights to others. Most home video distributors have their own direct mail capabilities, so this is unlikely.

Advance

The advance (sometimes called a ''*guarantee*'') is the money advanced to the program producer or rights holder in advance or in the expectation of the sales that the program will actually earn when it is released. That is not to say that just because you think your tape will sell 10,000 units that the distributor will pay an advance based on these projections. Different distributors use different methods of calculating the advance. Some distributors will base the advance on ''*out-of-the-box*'' projections (how many units are actually sold on the release date), since this is when the most sales are made. Other distributors estimate sales over a year or more and base the advance accordingly. Although it is an estimate at best, this gives some idea of what the program will be worth and how much it will generate in royalties. The advance is recoupable by the distributor and generally non-refundable if sales expectations are not met. Since it is money out of their pockets based on future sales, distributors do not look to give out high advances unless 1) your program is really terrific and sure to sell a lot of copies (by their judgment, not yours) or 2) distributors bid up the advance for the right to distribute the program. This seldom happens as there is so much product currently available.

Guarantee

A guarantee is payment from a distributor to the producer or rights holder and is also based on the earnings expectation of the program. Sometimes guarantees are paid up front, upon signing and delivery of the program to the distributor. At other times a guarantee is split up and paid out over a long period of time, regardless of the level of sales of the tape. It is normally not refundable. A guarantee is very similar to an advance and is generally recouped from royalties by the distributor.

Back End

In some cases a home video distributor will acquire other rights such as pay television, syndication, theatrical or other rights in the program. The contract will then usually specify that the distributor receive a distribution fee for each rights sale. The balance or ''*back end*'' is then shared using various formulae with the producer or rights holder.

Formats

Because there are several different formats available to consumers, the distribution contract will specify that your program will be duplicated in various formats, such as VHS, Beta, Laser, and 8mm. There may also be a clause that grants the rights to distribute in any new media that develops during the license period.

Royalty

Royalties are the monies that a producer receives from the sale and distribution of videocassettes. The definition of royalties is extremely critical and is negotiated by your lawyer. Sometimes royalties are defined as gross receipts: meaning all the monies (usually wholesale dollars) that are received by the distributor. In this case the producer or rights holder receives money from the first dollar (assuming the advance has been recouped by the distributor). In other cases, royalties are defined as accountable receipts, gross receipts less deductible amounts. Here the deductible amounts are specified and once they are deducted from the gross, the rights holder participates in a share of these monies.

Pricing

It is important to understand the pricing structure for home video in order to interpret the effects of royalty. The wholesale price is the price charged by a manufacturer (or as they are sometimes called, distributor) to the wholesaler. The wholesaler in turn sells the cassette to a dealer at a dealer's price. The video dealer or retailer may rent or sell the tape at a retail price to the consumer. In most instances a rights holder will receive a royalty based on monies received by a manufacturer, which is the wholesale price. Consequently if a tape sells for $59 (retail) the wholesale price is approximately $38. A 15% royalty of gross receipts (the wholesale price) would be $5.70. If the program sold for $39 at retail, then the wholesale price is approximately $24 and the 15% royalty would be $3.60. Although the manufacturer/distributor will set the price (and often lower it for re-release), by studying what they've done in the past with similar product, you will learn the expected retail price of your program. The higher the price, the more money you will receive.

Different distributors have different pricing structures and consequently your actual income may vary from distributor to distributor based on their pricing structure. In the above example, a 15% royalty of a $59 retail tape ($5.70) is more than 20% of a $39 tape at retail, which is $4.80. So comparing royalties between distributors is not enough to make a wise choice between them. You must understand how the pricing works in order to determine what you can expect in royalty dollars and base your projections accordingly.

Terms

Terms refers to the period of time in which the license agreement is in effect. Most distributors will want a long time period to recapture their advance and earn monies on the program. The distributor may require seven or 10 or more years as the term or license period.

Territories

Territories refers to the geographical locations where the distributor may sell the program. They can be specified as U.S. or U.S./Canada or Japan, and so forth. Sometimes the distributor will license worldwide rights. Some producers find a powerful worldwide distributor and make one deal. Others license off their programs to different distributors on a territory by territory basis. This is time consuming but sometimes yields more advance money. On the other hand, one distributor can coordinate an effective worldwide release using the same marketing materials. A coordinated worldwide release helps curb piracy. If the releases occur at the same time, a pirate will not have the opportunity to beat a distributor to the marketplace.

Overage

Overage is the term used for royalties received by the rights holder or producer once the advance has been recouped by the distributor. Sometimes an advance is recouped very quickly and at other times it may never be recouped. It all depends on the success of the program in the marketplace.

Return Allowance

The videocassette business is a packaged goods business. Although tapes may be sold and shipped and even paid for by the buyer, many distributors, in order to get their tapes out on the shelves, will guarantee that they'll take them back (returns) if they are not sold. When a distributor sells to a mass merchandiser, for example, provisions are made that require the distributor to take returns on tapes that are not sold. Consequently, a distributor could ship a large number of cassettes, only to find that six months down the road many would be returned. To avoid paying royalties on sales that really turn out to be returns, distribution contracts have a return allowance that holds back a small portion of royalties in case the program is returned. Once a certain period of time has elapsed and after any returns are made, this return allowance money is sent to the producer or rights holder.

Delivery Date

The delivery date is the specific time on or when the delivery of the master tapes and all other materials will occur. This date is part of the contract. The distributor needs to know the date in order to preplan a release date.

Holdbacks

Holdback is the period of time in which a program is withheld from other media. For example, a home video holdback is a period of time that the home video release is held back. If a film is playing theatrically, then obviously a home video release would hurt the box office so a holdback is specified. The home video holdback is usually lifted four to six months after the film has had its theatrical release. Once the home video period begins, there can be a pay TV holdback, meaning that the program cannot be shown on pay TV for a specified period of time. The same holds true for free TV, as broadcast of the program in free TV would diminish home video sales. It is important for a producer to understand the various windows or licensing periods in order to maximize potential income, so that he does not enter into agreements that may conflict with other distribution or licensing agreements.

Warranty

Any distribution agreement will contain a section regarding warranty. What this means is that the rights holder will represent to the distributor that he or she, the rights holder, has the right to grant the video rights, including all the literary, artistic, musical and other property rights, to the distributor. The rights holder will also assure the distributor that he will pay all charges, taxes, fees and other amounts that may be owed to the picture and that by entering into an agreement he will not infringe on any rights of any third party, and that if he does so, he will be responsible for any costs or legal fees. He also agrees that he, the rights holder, has not entered into any other agreements that may interfere with the grants being given to the distributor. He further assures the distributor that the program is copyrighted.

Materials

Materials refer to the elements that must be delivered to the distributor that enable the distributor to begin manufacturing the cassette, packaging and marketing materials. (A typical list is included later in this book.)

Indemnity

The rights holder indemnifies or holds harmless the distributor and the distributor's licensees, affiliates, employees and agents against any claims that may occur from other parties. He indemnifies the distributor against any costs arising from any breach of his representation or warranty. It is obvious that in the warranty and indemnification clauses, the producer must be very diligent in obtaining all rights to everything in the program from talent to music, so that no third parties come forth claiming rights in the program that endanger his agreement with the distributor.

Accounting Period

The accounting period refers to the time period after which the rights holder will receive a royalty statement. Some distributors report quarterly, some biannually and some annually. Normally the distributor will send a royalty report 45 to 60 days after the end of whatever time period is specified. Sometimes the accounting period can be staggered, such as quarterly for the first year and biannually thereafter, as most of the activity on a title currently comes within the first year of distribution.

Audit Rights

The rights holder may be granted audit rights, which give him the ability to audit the distributor's books during reasonable business hours in case of any dispute over royalties.

These are some of the major terms and issues that will come forth in negotiation. Discuss them with the distributor and your lawyer before concluding the deal.

THE CONTRACT

The Contract

''Negotiating is 'giving something, getting something.'''

Negotiating

Before we explore the deal itself, a little something about negotiating. Negotiating is an art; it's a skill. It is one of the most crucial moments before or after producing a program that really counts. Small points in a contract can make the difference between success and failure. If negotiations are approached in a methodical and careful manner, you should be able to obtain a fair and reasonable deal.

Webster defines negotiation as *''to confer, bargain, or discuss with a view to reaching agreement, to succeed in crossing, surmounting, moving through.''* Webster implies here that there will be some obstacles and difficulties, but that the basic premise of negotiating is that you are both agreeing to agree in the end. Negotiations can take many hours, many days or many months, depending on the litigiousness of your lawyer. Obviously the longer it takes to conclude a deal, the more expensive it will be (in lawyers' fees) and the longer it will take to get your program into distribution. However, negotiating is important and you should not rush through the process.

There is no way around negotiating. If you simply accept the distributor's *''standard contract,''* then you are accepting a contract that is written and designed by the distributor and may not necessarily reflect your best interests. Standard contracts can be rewritten and redrafted. A distributor will do this, however, only if he values your program. Consequently the more potential your program has in the marketplace, the more a distributor will want it and the more concessions he will make in order to give you a competitive and favorable deal.

If you are uncomfortable about negotiating, then have your lawyer or consultant do this for you. It is better to pay for someone to do this than to acquiesce because you are embarrassed to negotiate head-on. In other countries, negotiating is a way of getting involved with people. It is expected that one will barter back and forth before settling upon a price. It's part of the accepted social exchange. *Negotiate. Everything is negotiable.*

One thing you can do to enhance your position before negotiating is to collect information and to research contract elements. Reading and studying this book, consulting with your lawyer, talking with other producers who have made deals in home video, will assist in giving you more knowledge and information about the process. The more you know, the better you will do.

The negotiation process is one of *"giving something, getting something."* Both sides will enter into the negotiations expecting to win on some points and lose on others. Some points will be more valuable than others. You can always ask, although you may not receive, higher advances and royalties. But there is only so far a distributor is willing to go before he will walk away from the deal. You can test this point or limit by asking for more. For example, in negotiating a royalty you may ask for an escalation of that royalty once the cassette has sold a certain number of copies. For example, a 15% royalty until 50,000 sales, at which time the advance escalates to 17%, etc. The distributor may look for holdbacks in different media. It benefits the distributor to have an exclusive window on the sale and exploitation of cassettes without disruption by a free TV exposure. You benefit because more sales will be made until the program appears on TV. However, you may require the income from a television exhibition, and negotiate a shorter holdback.

Another example is, if you don't deliver artwork and color slides, then the distributor must have these made. It will cost $3,000 to prepare packaging. Depending on how much a distributor wants your program, he may or may not pay this amount without recouping it.

You may also request that a distributor pay for advertising and marketing, and specify the amount. In many cases this will show a distributor's good will. However, many distributors will not wish to specify an amount because they will spend whatever makes the most sense. If a program is no good and not accepted by the public, they will not want to spend additional monies. On the other hand, if it is successful they can put more money toward marketing, so this may be a moot point.

You can play distributors one off against the other and seek out the one who will pay you the highest advance or royalty, or make you the best overall deal. However, most distributors will not appreciate this game and you may lose a valuable relationship for future projects. Consequently it is better to pick the distributor you most want to be with and try to negotiate a favorable deal with your favorite distributor. This way everybody wins: You don't alienate your favorite distributor, and it leaves the door open for new projects in the future. If you try to get one bid from one distributor and then go to another and play the *let's-see-how-high-I-can-increase-the-bid* game, you may find distributors retracting their offer. No distributor wants to be leveraged into paying more than he thinks a program is worth.

You can ask for a performance clause in the contract, whereby a distributor must hit a certain number of sales before the license period will be extended. It won't always work, but maybe.

Initially you or your lawyer will deal with the acquisitions or program development person. The initial or broad strokes of the agreement will be set. A deal memo will then be sent on to the business affairs department or legal department of the distributor. Here the fine points and *"boilerplate"* will be worked out between your lawyer and the distributor's lawyer. There may be issues of language and definitions.

This may sound more difficult and cumbersome than it really is. Once you have gained experience with this process you will know what to ask for, what to fight for, and what to give up. Once you have negotiated an agreement with a distributor, it will make your second program easier to do because you will be able to gain everything you received in the first agreement and perhaps even more. If your program does well in the marketplace, then a distributor will want to work with you again and more favorable terms can be negotiated.

Consult with your lawyer, or find a lawyer who has dealt with the specific distributor you wish to negotiate with. This will enhance your opportunities.

Deal Memo

You've produced a terrific show. You've presented it to a distributor. The distributor likes it. Now what do you do?

At this stage three things can happen. The distributor can make you an offer verbally or in letter form. He can prepare a deal memo or deal letter. Or, if you agree to the basic terms, the distributor can go straight to contract.

An offer letter simply says that the distributor is interested in your show and will pay a specified advance and royalty. It is usually very brief and not terribly binding. This letter assures you there is interest, but unless it is written in hard legal terms and you are asked to sign it—as you would an agreement—it is really no more than a letter of interest. Some producers will go from one distributor to the next asking for written offers. Obviously, distributors do not like to do this because they know the producer is *"shopping the deal"* with other distributors. Their offer may only push their competitor to pay more; consequently, it's not in their best interests to write offers.

A producer who uses this approach generally alienates many distributors and is no longer a welcome face. However, if you only negotiated with one or two distributors (the ones you want to work with in the first place) and you intend to close a deal, make clear your intention, and then request a good faith offer letter. But then don't shop.

The program may also go to deal memo form. This deal memo may or may not be binding—but it usually is. In the deal memo, the basic terms are simply described: the show's title, the advance, the royalty, the terms or period of the license agreement, the territories and holdbacks if any. The memo is often one page long and written in simple terms. Usually the deal memo requires the producer's signature (or telex reply) confirming that both parties have agreed to the basic terms and will negotiate the standard contract terms in good faith at a later point. This assures both the distributor and the producer that the deal's a deal. Everyone can then relax.

Later the final points of the standard contract (the boilerplate) are worked out later between the distributor's attorney and the producer's attorney. A deal memo outlines the basic points and gives the producer's lawyer a place to start. Sometimes a lawyer or agent representing the producer will negotiate the deal memo in the producer's behalf. For a producer anxious to move into a distribution agreement, the deal memo is a way to expedite the process, as it is much easier and quicker to agree to a few simple points than a 15-page distribution contract. On the other hand, since a contract will ultimately be necessary anyway, the producer might as well go to full contract.

The formal contract can take days, weeks, or even months to negotiate. This is usually not so much a function of the contract's complexity, but rather the limited schedules of both the overworked entertainment attorney and the distributor's business affairs department, which has a never-ending stack of contracts to negotiate.

The Approach

When you first approach a distributor, you should allow a reasonable time for him to evaluate your project and respond—perhaps two or three weeks. If you try to apply pressure to the acquisition or development person to speed up the process, it may backfire. After all, it's much easier to say *"no"* than *"yes."* Besides, you are more familiar with the project, have spent months writing, or even longer producing it. The distributor needs time to view it and get up to speed. He also may simply be inundated with programs and proposals. (Our record number of proposals submitted at Vestron was nearly 200 in one week—and I expect that record to be broken before this book is printed.)

Often the decision on whether to acquire or produce a program does not rest with one person in the distribution company. Sales and marketing experts must be consulted. There may be release schedule considerations. There may be budgetary considerations. The distributor may need to assess how extensive a marketing campaign he will have to design and finance. There is a myriad of behind-the-scenes considerations that go into evaluating and ultimately selecting a program for distribution. You can help this process by providing stills, reviews, synopsis and pertinent background information about your program. Less is more. Do not sent too much. It will never be read. A one-page synopsis or highlights paragraph will be appreciated. Figure out how to sell your program in a few lines of copy. It will sell the acquisition person. The more promotable and marketable the show, the quicker a distributor will acquire it. You'll make his or her job easier, the program will sell well, and everyone will get credit for its success.

A sample distribution contract follows. This contract has been included in this book to prepare you for what a contract looks like, how to read, and what points it covers. This is not meant to be *"perfect"* or even represent a standard contract. Different distributors will have different ways of expressing the basic terms. Consult your lawyer. I accept no responsibility for any judgments you may make based on material in this book. (Unless of course your project is a smash success!) Nor am I suggesting any legal advice or consultation. This information is presented for your edification only. You should always have a lawyer negotiate and read your contracts before signing them. Good luck.

VIDEO DISTRIBUTION CONTRACT

AGREEMENT made as of July 25, 1985 between VIDEO INC. (''Distributor''), 1234 Money Lane, New York, New York 10012 and HOT SHOT PRODUCERS, a California corporation (''Grantor''), whose address is Box 1986, Hollywood, California 92645.

The parties hereby agree as follows:

1. Grant of Videocassette Rights: Grantor hereby grants to Distributor the sole and exclusive ''Videocassette Rights'' in the ''Picture.''

2. Picture: The ''Picture'' is the following:

''THE COUCH POTATO WORKOUT''

3. Definition of ''Videocassette Rights'': ''Videocassette Rights: means the right to include each Picture on ''Videocassettes'' manufactured during the ''Term'' in the ''Territory,'' and to exploit (by sale, lease or otherwise) such Videocassettes during and after the ''Term'' in the ''Territory''; provided, however, that such rights do not include (i) the right to authorize others to make a copy of any Videocassette that is manufactured for retail exploitation hereunder, or (ii) the right to publicly perform any Videocassette or to authorize others to do so; and provided further that remuneration for the transfer of possession of a Videocassette shall not be considered renumeration for the public performance thereof.

4. Definition of ''Videocassette'': ''Videocassette'' means a videocassette or

any other device, now or hereafter known or developed, that is capable of enabling a presentation of an audiovisual work to be perceived when used in combination with or as part of another piece of electronic, mechanical or other apparatus, or when used alone, and is primarily intended for "consumer" use, except that Videocassette shall not mean a so-called videodisc.

5. Term: In each country within the "Territory," the "Term" shall commence upon the execution hereof and shall expire at the close of the date seven years after completion of delivery pursuant to par. 7.

6. Territory: "Territory" means the United States, its territories and possessions (including Puerto Rico), and Canada. In addition, the Territory is deemed to include all ships and aircraft, wherever situated, that fly the flag of, are registered in, or book films in, the United States or Canada, and all camps, bases, sites and installations, wherever situated, that are owned, leased, used or occupied by the armed forces, governmental agencies, or public or private industrial or commercial concerns of the United States or Canada.

7. Delivery: Upon the execution of this Agreement, time being of the essence, Grantor shall make delivery of all items specified in, and otherwise fully comply with, the attached Exhibit A.

8. (a) Grantor's Participation: In full consideration of all rights granted herein and all services to be performed hereunder, Distributor will pay Grantor amounts ("Grantor's Royalties") equal to 15% of "Accountable Receipts," which shall be computed, determined and payable in accordance with and shall be subject to the attached Exhibit B. Promptly after the execution of this Agreement and the completion of delivery fully complying with paragraph 7, Distributor will pay Grantor an advance ("Recoupable Advance") of $10,000, which Distributor shall recoup from the payment of Grantor's Royalties. At such time as the Recoupable Advance has been recouped, all Grantor's Royalties shall thereafter be paid to Grantor.

(b) "Prototype Costs": Prototype costs means all of the direct out-of-pocket costs (such as for facilities, materials, services, and the use of equipment) in connection with all steps in the process leading to and including the production of the master Videocassettes that are made to serve as prototypes for the duplication of the Videocassettes of the Picture; each such cost shall be reimbursable when the obligation to pay for it is incurred or contracted, even if payment has not yet been made; if Distributor undertakes such process and in connection with such process Distributor furnishes any of its own facilities, materials, services or equipment for which Distributor has a standard rate, then the amount of such standard rate shall be deemed the amount of the applicable cost. If Distributor undertakes such process, Distributor shall notify Grantor in writing of the aggregate amount of the Prototype Costs of the Picture. Within 30 days after receipt of Distributor's notice setting forth such aggregate Prototype Costs, Grantor shall reimburse Distributor for one-half of such Prototype Costs up to $4,000, and all such Prototype Costs in excess of $4,000. In the event Grantor undertakes such process then, within 30 days after receipt of Grantor's notice setting forth the aggregate amount of the Prototype Costs of the Picture, Distributor shall reimburse Grantor for one-half of such Prototype Costs up to a maximum reimbursement of $2,000. In any event, all Prototype Costs in excess of $4,000 shall be Grantor's responsibility.

9. Instrument of Transfer: For purposes of copyright law, the instrument of transfer of the Videocassette Rights is deemed the document executed by Grantor contemporaneously herewith and following the form of the attached Exhibit C.

10. Warranties: Grantor hereby warrants and represents as follows:

(a) Grantor has the right to grant the Videocassette Rights herein, including but not limited to the necessary literary, artistic, musical, technological and/or intellectual property rights, and is free to enter into and fully perform this Agreement.

(b) Grantor has paid or will pay all charges, taxes, fees and other amounts that have been or may become owed in connection with the Picture or the exploitation of Videocassette Rights, and there are no pending claims, liens, charges, restrictions or encumbrances on the Picture or on the Videocassette Rights.

(c) The exercise of the Videocassette Rights will not infringe on any rights of any third party, including but not limited to copyright, patent, trademark, unfair competition, contract, defamation, privacy or publicity rights.

(d) Grantor has not granted or purported to grant, and will not grant or purport to grant, any Videocassette Rights or any other rights in the Picture or other audiovisual works that might derogate or interfere with the Videocassette Rights granted herein, and none of the Videocassette Rights in the Picture has ever been exploited by Grantor or any third party in the Territory.

(e) The Picture is currently protected by copyright in each country within the Territory.

(f) Distributor shall have the right to quiet and peaceful enjoyment of the Videocassette Rights.

11. Indemnity: Grantor shall at all times indemnify and hold harmless Distributor, its distributors, licensees, assignees and affiliated companies, and the officers, directors, employees and agents of all of the foregoing, against and from any and all claims, damages, liabilities, costs and expenses, including reasonable counsel fees, herein collectively called "claims," arising out of the exercise of the Videocassette Rights or any other rights hereunder, or out of any breach by Grantor of any representation, warranty or other provision hereof. If Distributor shall notify Grantor in writing of any claim, Grantor will promptly adjust, settle, defend or otherwise dispose of such claim at Grantor's sole cost. Unless Grantor has been so notified and is diligently and continuously pursuing such matter, Distributor may take such action on behalf of itself and/or attorney-in-fact for Grantor, to adjust, settle, defend or otherwise dispose of such claim, in which case Distributor may deduct from amounts otherwise due hereunder to Grantor all costs and expenses in connection therewith.

12. Incidental Rights: Distributor may not edit or modify any Picture or authorize others to do so. Distributor may translate, dub and/or subtitle any Picture, including but not limited to the title thereof, or authorize others to do so, and Distributor may include on any Picture, Videocassette or the packaging thereof the names and logos of Distributor and its licensees. No Picture shall appear alone on a Videocassette; Distributor shall include at least two of the Pictures on Videocassettes manufactured hereunder. Distributor may advertise, promote and publicize the Picture and the Videocassettes thereof in any media, or authorize others to do so; such advertising, promotion and publicity may include synopses or excerpts of the applicable Picture or pre-existing advertisements, publicity pieces and promotional materials, in whole or in part, for such Picture. Distributor may use and authorize others to use the name, likeness and voice of anyone who rendered services in connection with any Picture on the

packaging for any Videocassette of such Picture or for the purpose of advertising, promoting or publicizing such Picture or the Videocassettes thereof.

13. Miscellaneous: This Agreement contains the entire understanding and supersedes all prior understandings of the parties hereto relating to the subject matter herein, and this Agreement cannot be changed or terminated orally. Grantor will, upon Distributor's request, promptly furnish to Distributor copies of such agreements or other documents as Distributor may desire in connection with any provisions of this Agreement. This Agreement and all matters or issues collateral thereto shall be governed by the laws of the State of New York applicable to contracts executed and performed entirely therein.

IN WITNESS WHEREOF the parties hereto hereby execute this Agreement as of the date first specified above.

HOT SHOT PRODUCERS (''Grantor'')	VIDEO INC. (''Distributor'')
by________________________	by________________________

Exhibit A

Part of an Agreement dated as of July 25, 1985 between VIDEO INC. (''Distributor'') and HOT SHOT PRODUCERS (''Grantor'').

DELIVERY REQUIREMENTS

For each Picture, Grantor shall deliver the following items (''Delivery Materials'') to Distributor's address specified in this Agreement or such other address as Distributor shall specify:

1. In the case of production on film, a clean, unscratched composite 16 mm. release print of the Picture, in an aspect ratio of 1.33:1, made directly from a first generation CRI, or, in the case of production on video tape, a 1-inch VTR of the Picture, made directly from the complete original master VTR; provided, however, that if the Picture was not originally produced in an English-language

version, then the print or VTR shall be of an English-language dubbed version of the earliest generation available. Upon Distributor's request, at any time during the Term, Grantor shall deliver any other then-existing version of the Picture, including, but not limited to, any dubbed or subtitled version in any foreign language.

2. A reasonable quantity of pre-existing advertisements, publicity pieces and promotion materials, including as a minimum but not limited to:

(i) a sufficient amount of color artwork (whether in the form of slides, chromes, posters or otherwise) to enable Distributor to produce satisfactory packaging of the Videocassette; and

(ii) a reasonable quantity of black-and-white and color stills (with notations of the persons and subject matter appearing in such stills).

3. A synopsis of the advertising credits that were used for distribution in other media.

4. A list of the principal performers in the Picture and the functions they perform.

5. A music cue sheet in customary form containing titles, composers, timings, copyright owners and publishers.

6. A copy of the proper copyright notice.

Grantor warrants that all Delivery Materials shall be suitable in all respects for all uses thereof contemplated herein.

Exhibit B

Part of an Agreement dated as of July 25, 1985 between VIDEO INC. (''Distributor'') and HOT SHOT PRODUCERS (''Grantor'').

ACCOUNTABLE RECEIPTS

I. ''Accountable Receipts'': ''Accountable Receipts'' means ''Gross Receipts'' less ''Deductible Amounts.'' Accountable Receipts, Gross Receipts and all Deductible Amounts shall be calculated as of the close of the applicable ''accounting period'' (as hereinafter defined) on a cumulative basis for such accounting period and all prior accounting periods.

II. ''Gross Receipts'': ''Gross Receipts'' means 100% of moneys actually received by Distributor in U.S. dollars in the United States from the exploitation of Videocassette Rights in the Picture, except that in the case of direct mail transactions ''Gross Receipts'' means 50% of such monies. Monies actually received by Distributor are at all times subject to retroactive adjustment, such as for returns, refunds, credits, settlements, allowances, rebates and discounts; provided, however, that in connection with the exploitation of Videocassette Rights in the Picture in the ''Foreign Area,'' ''Accountable Receipts'' means 60% of monies actually received by Distributor's wholesaler (computed after the deduction of any Value Added Tax and subject to adjustments, returns, refunds and discounts). ''Domestic Area'' means the United States and its territories and possessions (including Puerto Rico). ''Foreign Area'' means the rest of the Territory excluding the Domestic Area.

III. Deductible Amounts: ''Deductible Amounts'': means the sum of the following:

(i) all sales, gross receipts, turnover, foreign withholding, excise, use and personal property or similar taxes levied upon, payable with respect to, or arising in connection with the exploitation, use, distribution, revenues, or materials of the Videocassettes of the Picture, but specifically excluding any net income, corporate franchise or excess profits tax; and

(ii) all costs of converting, transmitting, or remitting currency.

IV. Statements and Payments: ''Accounting period'' means each of the 6-month periods beginning on any January 1st and July 1st (except that Distributor may at any time elect to use other 6-month periods). Within 90 days after the end of each accounting period, Grantor shall be sent a statement showing the computation of Accountable Receipts for such accounting period and Grantor shall be paid the Grantor's Royalties (if any) based thereon. No statement need be sent for any accounting period in which there are no Gross Receipts. Any withholding or deduction required by law may be made.

V. Conclusiveness of Statements: Distributor shall keep all of its books and records directly relating to this Exhibit in accordance with accepted accounting principles. Grantor may, at Distributor's offices and for reasonable times within regular business activities, but not more than once per calendar year, have a certified public accountant inspect and make copies of any such books and records not previously inspected, all at Grantor's expense. Each such inspection shall be completed within 30 consecutive days. Distributor's method of treating any amount referred to in this Exhibit for Distributor's tax or financial purposes will have no bearing on the computation of Accountable Receipts. Each statement hereunder shall be deemed conclusive unless Grantor shall object thereto to Distributor in writing within 18 months after receipt thereof and shall state in detail in such writing the basis for the objection. Grantor shall be barred from bringing any legal proceeding on the subject matter of such objections later than 12 months after making such objections If any figures on a statement re-appear on, or are included in cumulative amounts on any later statement, the later statement shall be disregarded in computing Grantor's time to object or to bring legal proceedings.

VI. Foreign Currency: If any foreign government shall block the conversion or transmittal of currency to be included in Gross Receipts, Distributor, in its sole discretion may pay, or if Grantor so requests in writing Distributor shall pay, Grantor's Royalties applicable to such Gross Receipts by depositing the same in Grantor's name and at Grantor's expense with such depository in the applicable country as Grantor shall designate, all of which is subject to such laws, rules and regulations as may be applicable to such deposits.

VII. Relationship of Parties: Distributor shall not be deemed a fiduciary, partner or joint venturer of Grantor, and may assign this Agreement or any rights or obligations hereunder. Any pledge, hypothecation, mortgage, or other encumbrance of any Picture, or any assignment, sale or transfer of rights herein, purported to be made by or on behalf of Grantor, shall be void; provided, however, that after the completion of Grantor's delivery of the Picture in accordance with this Agreement any assignment, sale or transfer of Grantor's right to receive Grantor's Royalties under this Agreement shall be valid if it shall be made specifically subject to Distributor's rights herein, and Distributor's payment of Grantor's Royalties to the assignee, buyer or transferee shall be subject to the execution of Distributor's standard form of payment authorization. Grantor waives any right to purport to terminate the Videocassette Rights in the Picture or to pursue any remedies in connection with this Agreement other than a suit for money damages. No entity that owns or controls, is owned or controlled by, or is under common ownership or control with Distributor shall be considered as an agent for or as the same entity as Distributor. As between Grantor and Distributor, Distributor shall have sole discretion: to make a fair allocation of any Gross Receipts or Deductible Amounts from any larger sums in which they are included; to determine whether to incur any cost that is a Deductible Amount, when it is incurred, and how it is computed; to determine when the conversion or transmittal of currency shall occur and the exchange rate at which such conversion shall occur; to determine the parties, sale price and all other terms of such agreement, if any, for the exploitation of Videocassette Rights; to settle any claim with respect to any such agreement, any Videocassettes, or the Videocassette Rights; to distribute free or promotionally Videocassettes; to destroy or erase Videocassettes; to set up reasonable reserves for reasonable amounts of time; and to commingle funds applicable to payments hereunder with other funds. Distributor makes no representation or warranty with respect to Distributor's efforts in connection with the exploitation of Videocassette Rights or that such exploitation will result in any minimum amount of Gross Receipts, Accountable Receipts, or Grantor's Royalties.

Exhibit C

Part of an Agreement dated as of July 25, 1985 between VIDEO INC. (''Distributor'') and HOT SHOT PRODUCERS (''Grantor'')

INSTRUMENT OF TRANSFER

For One Dollar ($1.00) and other good and valuable consideration, the receipt of which is hereby acknowledged, the undersigned (''Grantor'') hereby assigns to VIDEO INC. (''Distributor''), by means of this instrument of transfer, the sole and exclusive rights (subject to such rights becoming non-exclusive in accordance with the provisions of the agreement referred to in the next paragraph) to manufacture ''Videocassettes'' of the following audiovisual work during the ''Term'' in the ''Territory,'' and to exploit (by sale, lease or otherwise) such Videocassettes during and after the ''Term'' in the ''Territory''; provided, however, that such rights do not include (i) the right to authorize others to make a copy of any Videocassette that is manufactured for retail exploitation hereunder, or (ii) the right to publicly perform any Videocassette for remuneration or to authorize others to do so; and provided further that remuneration for the transfer of possession of a Videocassette shall not be considered renumeration for the public performance thereof. Such Picture is at present entitled:

THE COUCH POTATO WORKOUT

"Videocassette" means a videocassette or any other device, now or hereafter known or developed, that is capable of enabling a presentation of an audiovisual work to be perceived when used in combination with or as part of another piece of electronic, mechanical or other apparatus, or when used alone, and is primarily intended for "consumer" use except that Videocassette shall not mean a so-called videodisc. "Territory" means the United States, its territories and possessions (including Puerto Rico), and Canada. In each country within the Territory, the "Term" shall commence upon the execution hereof and shall expire at the close of the date seven years after completion of delivery pursuant to paragraph. 7.

This instrument of transfer is executed in connection with and is subject to an agreement between Grantor and Distributor, dated as of July 25, 1985.

HOT SHOT PRODUCERS
("Grantor")

by______________________________

COUNTY OF ___________________________)
)SS.
STATE OF ____________________________)

On this ________ day of __________________________ 19 ____, before me personally came____
to me known, who being by me duly sworn did depose and say that he is the ______________________________________ of HOT SHOT PRODUCERS, the corporation described in and which executed the above instrument; that he knows the seal of said corporation; that the seal affixed to said instrument is such corporate seal; that it was so affixed by order of the Board of Directors of said corporation; and that he signed his name hereunto by like order.

____

NOTARY PUBLIC

Delivery Requirements

Your contract is signed and now the producer is expected to make delivery of certain materials before the advance is paid, which may include:

One-Inch Master

Producers should contact the distributor's production department to make sure that the 1-inch videotape master will conform to the specifications necessary for duplication. In most cases, the distributor will want a submaster from your master edited version. In the U.S., an NTSC master is required. International duplication requires PAL and to a lesser degree SECAM formats. Most distribution contracts have a separate page that specifies the technical requirements for the 1-inch master. Once delivered, the distributor will have the master checked for quality (quality control). Once it is approved, the distributor will notify the business affairs department who will see that a check for the advance is issued also assuming all other materials required are also delivered. Do not expect to deliver your master and be paid a check the same day. Be aware that masters are most frequently rejected because there are glitches on the tape, or the film print was dirty before it was transferred, or there are drop outs in the sound. Don't expect approval on a poor master; you'll only be wasting time. Besides, you will want the tapes that are ultimately released to be of the finest quality.

Trailer

Many distributors require that a 60-second trailer, or coming attractions reel be delivered. The trailer is used to market the film to wholesalers and retailers. Feature film producers have often already produced a trailer using the best shots from the film to whet the viewers appetite.

Original programs will require carefully constructed trailers emphasizing their value to the retailer (and consumer). Since the distributor will probably have a better sense of how to position and market your program, he may make the trailer and recoup these costs from royalties. If you are required to deliver a trailer, check with the marketing department of the distribution company to make sure that you deliver something consistent with its marketing plans. Do not make your trailer without consulting with someone or the distributor may ask you to redo it. The best approach will be to develop the script and off-line trailer edit with the distributor.

Artwork/Color Slides/Stills

The distributor needs artwork to use in the packaging and marketing of the videocassette. Color stills are frequently used on both the cassette jacket and promotional one-sheets. If your color stills are of hosts or leading stars, make sure to deliver the color slides that have been approved by the talent (if the talent has approval). Do not deliver slides that have not been cleared, as lawsuits can ensue. Black and white stills will be used for promotion and publicity. Artwork—such as that used in a theatrical or television campaign—may also be required.

Credits

Production credits will be printed on the front or back of the cassette package. This varies as each distributor has his own packaging style. Supply three to five credits for the stars, director, producer, writer, etc. Use the correct spellings. If you don't, no one else will either.

Synopsis

Prepare a one- or two-paragraph synopsis of your program. This most likely will be used, re-edited and rewritten by the marketing department for the back of the package. It will also be used by the publicity department when writing press releases. Include any bios of any principal players or creative talent involved with the project.

Script

If you have made a worldwide distribution deal, then the distributor will require a script. The script should have a shot list in the left-hand column and dialogue or narration in the right-hand column. This script is then translated and re-recorded against picture. Sometimes this script is used to create subtitles for the program. Each foreign territory differs; some will dub, some will use subtitles.

M & E Tracks

If your program is dubbed, the distributor will need an M&E *(music and effects)* track. This is a mix of your sound track excluding dialogue and narration. This track, together with the new dubbed voices is mixed for the foreign version. Again, check with the distributor's production department to make sure that your M&E track is prepared to its specifications. If it isn't, and you make assumptions, you may be asked to do it over again, which will delay your payment.

Music Cue Sheet

A sheet listing all the musical elements, publishers and composers and running times of the music will also be requested.

Copyright

You may be asked to submit a copy of your copyright form. This you can obtain for a small fee ($10) from the Library of Congress, Copyright Office, Washington, D.C. Ask for form PA (Performing Arts). It may take several weeks to get the form, so apply when your program is in the final stages of editing. If the distributor has produced the program or fully financed the program, he will copyright it in his name and you won't be required to submit this form.

Backing Documents

Backing documents are those release forms, stock footage releases, and music rights clearances and any other release that covers all the rights within your program. Some distributors will ask for copies of these documents to assure that there is no infringement on a third party's rights. These will be submitted to the insurance company as well with your E&O application.

E&O Insurance

As discussed previously, E&O insurance is errors and omissions insurance. Many distributors will require this insurance policy for any program they acquire. To protect themselves, they will not release any program that does not have E&O. This policy protects the distributor if any third party comes forward and justifiably requires a rights payment.

These are the primary delivery requirements for most programs. Some distributors will require fewer materials; others will require more. Find out early on in your discussions with the distributor what he will require so that you will have time to assemble them. Even if something is not contractually required, like promotional stills, it doesn't hurt to provide them. Any help you can give the distributor will be beneficial to the promotion of your program.

The message here is to know in advance what will be required of you so that you can prepare and deliver it in a timely fashion. This will benefit you because the faster you deliver approved materials, the faster you will get your advance check.

SELF-DISTRIBUTION

Self-Distribution

''For every success story there are dozens who have failed at self-distribution.''

Self-Distribution

At some time in every film producer's career, he has asked himself if, given the opportunity, could he do a better job distributing the program than a distributor? Producers are sometimes concerned that large distributors have so much product that programs may get lost, or conversely, with small distributors, they don't have enough clout or financing to successfully market their programs. Or, sometimes, after a thorough search, a producer finds that a distributor may not handle a specific program. Producers then think of self-distribution as an alternative.

My own feeling is that if you have produced a commercial viable program, one that can succeed in the traditional video outlets, then it is best to go with your favorite established distributor.

Whether you are a large traditional distributor or a small self-distributor, the challenge is the same: How do you get your tape in front of the desired audience? If, as a self-distributor, you are trying to reach the video retail trade, the mom-and-pop stores, then most likely you would use wholesalers just like the big guys. The only difficulty is that the wholesalers also wish to make a profit and only take on programs they think they can sell successfully. A second problem arises when you are distributing only one or two programs. You don't have the desired *''A''* titles to leverage wholesalers into taking your *''B''*, *''C''*, and *''D''* product. Furthermore, you may have trouble collecting from a wholesaler whose dollars go first to his most important suppliers—the ones who can consistently bring him moneymaking titles.

If, on the other hand, you have a specialized program designed for a specific audience, and you have the knowledge, ability and enthusiasm to go after this audience, either through direct mail or magazine space advertising, self-distribution might be worthwhile. If this is the case, you then must design a marketing, promotion, distribution and fulfillment campaign for the program and follow through on it. Something to consider: If you self-distribute you are taking your attention away from producing. You have to ask yourself, *"What do I really want to do?"*

If you have identified your target audience as, let's say, equestrian, then you can advertise your tape in equestrian magazines and newsletters, acquire a mailing list of all the horse owners, seek out equestrian clubs and events, etc. A test mailing can determine whether or not they will buy your tape before you invest a lot of money in a full-scale campaign.

The secret to success in marketing your tape is to know exactly who your market is. Dr. Art Ulene, who is well known from his frequent appearances on *The Today Show* produced a series of tapes including one on *Childbirth Preparation* (adopted by LaMaze), a *Pregnancy* and a *Post-Natal Exercise* program. These tapes sold for $39.95. They were distributed through the *American Society of Pediatricians and Obstetricians* newsletter (11,000 circulation), through doctor's offices, LaMaze classes, bookstores, motherhood and maternity stores, pharmacies, traditional video wholesalers and through direct mail ads in magazines like *Family Circle*. Furthermore, Art Ulene toured various cities to promote the series of tapes. He knew his audience and marketed a well-produced tape. The package let consumers know that it was approved by the *American College of Obstetricians* so they felt they could trust its contents. Every *"element for success"* was fully exploited in the way the tape and marketing was put together: 1) Art Ulene is a well-known name, 2) he was willing to tour and promote the tapes, 3) LaMaze and the American College of Obstetricians brought credibility to the content, 4) they were well-produced programs, 5) the marketing campaign was highly efficient and targeted, 6) he released a series of tapes so they could be cross-promoted and costs amortized. These self-distributed and marketed tapes sold exceedingly well. In this case, it was unlikely that a traditional distributor would know how to effectively market and distribute these tapes through these alternative and very specialized outlets.

Another self-distribution success story comes from Bob Katz and Jerry Turner. They sold more than 5,000 copies of two travel ski tapes in Colorado alone!

However, beware. For every success story there are dozens who have failed at self-distribution. It's a shame to see these tapes delivered by the barrelful to Vestron for distribution consideration. The producers spent money on the production, and on packaging and a marketing campaign, and failed and now are looking to bail out. But few distributors will handle a tape that has already been unsuccessfully exploited. Most of these people didn't research the marketplace, produce a tape of any salable or rentable value, or have any idea how to market their tapes.

When you self-distribute, you can receive a greater return than a small royalty (15%-20% of the gross), but you will spend much of your income on expenses beyond the production budget, such as advertising, marketing, the printing of flyers, creation of artwork, advertising, overhead, phone, freight, accounting, legal fees, duplication and packaging. You are a manufacturer and must be concerned with packaging, marketing and fulfillment, which take significant time and commitment. This will probably not be worth your time unless you have a tape that can realistically sell 1,000 units or more at a relatively high price, and/or have more than one title. The economics simply may not work out.

Draw up a business plan before leaping into the distribution business. Can you really do it? Who is your competition? Are there other distributors who have successfully distributed a limited number of titles? Research costs, get quotations from duplicators, really learn what wholesalers, retailers and consumers pay for tapes and whether yours is one that they may wish to buy. Making the wrong assumptions can put you out of business in a hurry.

In marketing your program, you will have to determine a price that is competitive with other tapes in the same genre. If you are looking to sell your tape, and it is truly a sell-through kind of product, then you will have to set a price that is appropriate. If you are selling directly to a highbrow public, then it is possible that you can charge high prices. On the other hand, if you are hoping to sell through direct mail or magazines to the general public, then the price should be low, thus reducing your opportunity for significant profits. You will probably find it extremely difficult to compete with the 400-500 titles that are being released each month by manufacturers.

Most manufacturers distribute their programs through a variety of outlets and so it would be unusual for one to give up direct mail, but let's suppose that you find one who agrees to cover the traditional outlets and lets you retain the direct mail market. If you know your audience and how to reach it, it might be worthwhile. Of course, the sequencing of the direct mail release must be coordinated so as not to damage sales in the traditional markets. Prices will also need to be consistent.

Duplication costs will never be as low for a small distributor as they are for a large distributor. It's simply a question of volume. After the program and art work mechanicals are produced there are also the manufacturing costs of cassette and duplication, jacket artwork, labels, antipiracy stickers, and freight. Since duplication prices have been falling and vary greatly with volume orders between manufacturers, you should contact various duplicators to bid on your job. (A list of some duplicators is provided in the back of the book.)

Before embarking on self-distribution, contact other self-distributors. You can do this by looking at the home video consumer magazines and noting the ads that offer sell-through product. Contact these self-video publishers and ask how they have organized their business. It is a considerable commitment, but if you have a tape with a specific market and you can reach that market, then you should have success. An important question to ask yourself is, *''Do I really want to be in the distribution business?''* Most producers don't.

MARKETING

Marketing

"Video retailers are the core of home video, but others have entered with gusto."

Traditional Video Stores

The traditional video store began the home video rental business. It caught on in a big way. VCR owners, looking to do something besides time-shift, began renting tapes. There are about 20 large and 80 to 100 small program suppliers who supply a network of wholesalers who in turn sell to the video stores.

As discussed before, the 25,000 traditional video stores are primarily in the rental business. Some are beginning to offer tapes for sale but most of their income (75%) presently comes from rentals even though the *1985 Video Software Dealers Association (VSDA)* has been encouraging stores to increase their efforts to sell programs. The video retailer is the core of home video today but other retailers have entered with gusto with sell-through product.

Record Stores

Until Michael Jackson's videotape *Thriller*, record stores did not sell video tapes. In a few months after its release, more than 2,500 record stores sold music video. Today there are about 1,000 stores that sell music video on a regular basis, mostly at $29.95 and less. Even though there are more than 10,000 record stores in the U.S., only 10% sell video. Expectations are that as prices fall, and second machines come into the homes, this number will expand significantly in the next few years.

Although music video has not fulfilled early golden promises (few have sold over 50,000 units), its day will come. And when it does, the logical place for sell-through music product is the record store.

Today's major record store retailers that sell music videos are *Camelot, Harmony, Hastings, Wherehouse, Licorice Pizza, Musicland/Sam Goody's, Record World,* and *Tower*.

A 1985 survey by the *National Association of Recording Merchandisers* indicated that sales of prerecorded cassettes accounted for 62.2% of video revenue, and video rentals accounted for 33.8% of the record stores' video dollar volume.

When the VCR penetration is similar to that of audio tape players among teenagers, there will be an explosion of music video product being sold through record stores.

Bookstores

More than any other new outlet, bookstores offer a tremendous opportunity for well-selected original programs. At present there are only a few bookstore chains committed to selling video tapes. (Bookstores do not rent tapes.) Bookstores have carried anywhere from 20 to 50 titles, generally best sellers or titles with names that have some identification among book browsers. One should expect to see this change as consumers learn that they can buy videotapes on a wide range of subjects at low prices in bookstores. Paperbacks are a natural for bookstores, and specialty programs will be, too.

Karl/Lorimar's home video *Eat to Win* received heavy promotion in bookstores along with the best-selling book of the same title. Vestron's *Treasure* was similarly cross-promoted.

Producers developing product for the bookstores should first develop a marketing plan, so that they know before the cameras roll whether the tape meets the needs of retail bookstores.

Book publishers, distributors and librarians are all excited by the possibility of video in bookstores. *Waldenbooks* has placed videos in 891 of its stores, *B. Dalton* in 729, and *Hastings* in 150. This represents only 1,800 stores of a possible retail book trade universe of 15,000 (21,525 in total). Waldenbooks expects more than 1,000 bookstores to carry video in 1986 with each store selling 12 to 300 titles. Its video revenue in 1985 tripled its 1984 sales. Presently audio and video make up about 18% of Waldenbooks' total dollar volume. With results like that, it won't be long before it is commonplace to see videotapes in bookstores everywhere.

Kartes, a video distributor and manufacturer, has made significant impact in the book trade, and sells a line of public domain classic movies in about 2,000 stores. Jim Kartes, president, says that the company has sold about 700,000 units through bookstores alone. These sales were made at the *American Booksellers Association (ABA)* in Washington and San Francisco in the past few years. Sales of public domain titles have fallen off but allowed Kartes to gain a valuable toe-hold among the book trade to distribute new titles including *How to Pick Up Men* ($19.95), *Peak Performance, Zorro's Fighting Legions* (a 12-part series), *Keystone Comedies* (eight volumes) and *Arf,* a 30-minute original title for dogs (really!) with a sound track of barking and music ($9.95—how many dogs do you know with that kind of money?). Other titles sold in bookstores include Paramount's *Strong Kids, Safe Kids* and Karl's legendary *Jane Fonda Workout*. Stuart Karl, president of Karl/Lorimar Home Video, says that *"50% of the future of the home video business lies with the bookstores."* Low price collectibles such as Paramount's *Star Trek,* Disney animations, MGM's *"Great Books,"* and Vestron's *National Geographic* have all been successful. Well-known book publishers have entered the video business by producing, acquiring and distributing programs such as Random House's *Julia Child Cooking* series, Simon and Schuster's *Sherlock Holmes* and *The Jewel in the Crown* series and Western Publishing's *Golden Books*.

Bookstores like to see home video priced as low as possible: $29.95, $24.95, $19.95, $14.95, or less is the right price.

Western priced its *Golden Books* video line in the $8.95-$9.95 range. It shipped over 1 million of the first eight titles, and expects to exceed 2 million units. The line is carried by about 30,000 video outlets, including many bookstores.

Other examples are Addison-Wesley's *Esquire* cassettes, *Raquel Welch: Total Fitness and Beauty* (Thorn/EMI) with a book by Holt Rinehart and Winston. Acropolis licensed its book rights to Kartes for *Color Me Beautiful* and *The Eight Minute Makeover*. The books sold well; the videos did not.

Bookstores look for solid hits—be they movies or exercise. Other program genres that will emerge will be education, information, magazines and calendars, classic movies, health, children's and music, but a promotable hook will continue to be important as well as repeatability and collectability.

The 1984 Gallup poll lists these genres as most popular, in descending order, among book buyers: mystery, suspense, romance, popular fiction, historical, action/adventure, science fiction, western, humor, occult/supernatural, war/military. The same poll lists the best-selling nonfiction genres to be: reference/instruction, biography, religious, health/diet, exercise, home and garden how-to, leisure, investment/income tax. Do the same genres follow for home video programming?

One factor that has slowed down the availability of video in bookstores is that they expect a margin of 45% or more, and long lead times for orders. This strains the video manufacturer who is not accustomed to such margins. Also, video manufacturers announce new titles about two months in advance of release and expect orders. Bookstores and mass merchandisers order quarterly. What's happening is that two different businesses are learning how to work with each other. Over time, compromises will be made on both sides, VCR penetration will continue to increase and more product will find a home on booksellers' shelves. Video into bookstore outlets has just begun. Every success will open up this channel of distribution even further.

Toy Stores

Toy stores are an exciting new outlet for video product. Obviously most of the programming is for children or the family. Unless it is a game, it is sold at low prices, $29 or less. The 1984 toy market represented $10 billion in sales, 70% of which was received in the last quarter of the year. In the U.S. there are 375 super toy stores, such as the *Toys 'R Us* chain, and 1,200 toy specialty outlets. All are potential markets for children's video sales. Other major players are *Child World, Circus World,* and *Lionel Leisure*. Many are selling Western's Golden Book video line for under $29.95. In the next few years, low-cost VCRs will encourage second machines to be brought into the home, further driving up the sale of children's software. As a genre, children's video is the largest-growing non-movie form of programming.

Toys 'R Us is one of the most aggressive merchandisers of videotapes. It sells such titles as: *Rainbow Brite* and *My Little Pony* from Vestron's Children's Video Library, $29.95, seven of the Western titles, the *Care Bears, Transformers* and *G.I. Joe* (Family Home Entertainment), *Charlie Brown,* three volumes (Media Home Entertainment), seven Disney titles priced between $18 and $28, and public domain titles such as *Bugs Bunny, Felix the Cat, Mr. Ed,* and *W.C. Fields* from Kids Classics at $9.95. Coliseum is selling four wrestling tapes in *Toys 'R Us* at $49.95. (Few retailers have probably viewed this product!)

One of the most successful programs has been *Clue,* a videotape game from Parker Brothers. Parker shipped more than 100,000 units when the tape was first released. The company has sold over 300,000 to date, about 90% to toy stores—and not the traditional video retailer. Toys 'R Us was the biggest single buyer. The program is priced at $39.95.

Children's video business in the toy trade could represent $25 million at wholesale. This may increase to $50 million by the end of 1986 when toy stores take on additional entertaining and educational tapes. Many mass merchandisers, such as *Venture, Bradlee's* and *Hallmark,* carry tapes in their children's departments. *Toys 'R Us* says the average parent spends $170 a year on toys. About half these purchases are impulse buys. Toy stores favor cassettes, often prepackaged in blisterpacks and displayed on peg board hangers, that feature pre-promoted, recognizable characters. As programmers, distributors and toy retailers gain more experience, the business will be even greater than it is today.

Initially, there was some resistance to selling video in toy stores, because the chains weren't accustomed to dealing with the video vendors. For example, toy stores do not order video every month, which is the norm with video retailers. Also, toy stores expect higher return policies and greater profit margins, which video manufacturers are reluctant to give. But over time these differences will be worked out and everyone will prosper.

Convenience, Drug and Grocery Stores

Convenience stores and supermarkets are ideal places to rent and sell videocassettes. Customers are by nature return customers, and the rental occurs at a place they are accustomed to visiting frequently. Customers, mostly women, come in throughout the day; men shop at night. Since they return to the store frequently, it provides an opportunity to return tapes and rent new ones. There have been many experiments in supermarkets and convenience stores, including *Kroger, Safeway,*

Lucky, ShopRite, Winn-Dixie, Wegmans, Dominicks, H. E. Butt, King Soopers, Publix, Albertson's, Alpha Beta, Schnuck's, Randall's, Shaw's, Purity Supreme, and *Pathmark* among others. More stores handling video have been at rural, not the urban, locations where video is already available through traditional rental stores. On the average, a store may gross between $300 and $1,500 per week. The additional income is important, but they also want to lure return customers.

There is an estimated universe of 40,000 drug, food and convenience stores. Some of the current major players are *Jack Eckhart* with 1,000 stores, *Fotomat* with 3,000, *Safeway* 2,500, *7-Eleven* with 6,000, and *Rite Aid* with 12,000. Among the majors, there is a potential of more than 14,000 stores. At present there are about 6,000 convenience stores that carry video to some degree, a tremendous leap from two years ago when only 600 carried video. *C-Store, Southland's 7-Eleven* and *Circle K* are the big players. Each store carries about 250 to 400 titles, mostly hits. Stores figure not only will they create a new profit center and encourage customer returns but make food sales as well.

Some tests are taking place in convenience stores with automated vending machines. At present there are only a few thousand in operation. With some machines you can use a credit card to rent tapes. When they are returned, the credit card down payment is deleted from the statement. It is too early to tell whether these machines will prove successful in the marketplace. The convenience stores are ideally positioned to make a significant impact in the video rental business.

Video Clubs

It would make sense that videos can be sold the same way books can, and hence one would think there is a proliferation of video clubs. But only a handful of companies have been successful. *CBS Records' Columbia House and Time Inc.'s Book of the Month Club* have both seen success with the sale of videos through club membership. With a large mailing list, they have both been able to make sales to collectors of videotapes. In the late '70s, when video first became available, there were many companies that tried and failed at direct marketing through mail order. There simply wasn't a large enough base of customers to make these ventures cost effective. Such companies as *Time/Life Films, VCA, Fotomat, Magnetic Video,* and several others tried and failed when club members found that it was easier to rent a tape from their local video store than to order it by mail. Americans want it and they want it now! Also VCR owners are not necessarily the people that buy video by mail. *Cambridge Associates,* a research firm, estimates that by 1988, direct mail will constitute about 15% of the video business. In 1985 it was 3% of gross video revenues.

Crown Publishers recently began to offer a line of videos through their book catalogs. The titles are selected and culled from many independent distributors.

Time's Book of the Month Club sells older public domain and nostalgic compilations. It has about 2 million members. Doubleday also has a specialty video club, which specializes in war films.

CBS Video Club is the direct mail company of CBS Records. It has more than 100,000 members participating in a negative option plan. Consumers buy the first cassette for about $5 with an option for a second cassette at $30. For this special offer they must buy two more cassettes at full price during the next year. With every purchase, new members are entitled to the next cassette at half price. The club reaches VCR owners through direct mail and space ads in magazines and newspapers. It sells everything from old film classics to music videos, exercise tapes and instructional tapes. Its catalog is sent out about once a month and contains theatrical and children's titles as well. It has sold some specialty titles and is beginning to offer more non-movie product. The club has been successful with instructional product and documentary films and specializes in programs that are not distributed by the video stores, thereby providing a service that the video stores cannot.

The club also offer the continuity series, *World War II,* through *CBS Video Library* to some 25,000 members. Here is an entire series of tapes on a single theme—sold on an ongoing basis. Members buy the first tape at about $5 and then receive subsequent volumes at the full price of $49 about every other month until they say they've had enough or have collected them all. During mid-1985 CBS also released a *Vietnam War* series, narrated by Walter Cronkite, and an *I Love Lucy* series.

The video club tends to work well for non-feature programming and programs that are not readily found elsewhere. Once a devoted membership is built, the marketing group can reach the consumer easily and quickly. The difficulty with such video club programs is the enormous start-up costs involved. Ongoing costs such as acquisition, production, catalog printing, and mailing are enormously expensive, but once a company has mined a specialized audience through video clubs, sales can be very profitable.

Magazine Space Ads

Videocassettes are also marketed through space ads in magazines. While this isn't exactly a market unto itself, it is a delivery system that can be effective to a targeted and select audience. *Lords of the Ring* and *Ringmasters,* two wrestling tapes from Vestron, were sold through traditional outlets as well as space ads in *Pro Wrestling Illustrated* magazine (also one of the sponsors of the program). *Weight Watchers Guide to a Healthy Lifestyle* (Vestron) was advertised to the Weight Watcher community through *Weight Watchers Magazine. Esquire's* six lifestyle cassettes were advertised through *Esquire* magazine display ads. When a producer can identify an audience and produce a program through a specific magazine and then advertise in that magazine, he will have an effective tool in successfully reaching an interest audience for the tape.

National Geographic Video series is advertised in issues of *National*

Geographic Magazine. The demographics reveal that more than 40% of National Geographic members have VCRs. Space ads and direct mail are therefore very effective in selling the programs. Producers should be careful in identifying magazines with the appropriate demographics for videotape sales. For example, it is unlikely that high-priced videocassettes can be sold through teen-age magazines. Teenagers at present do not have VCR machines or money to spend on tapes. A producer or distributor would consequently be wasting money advertising to a market such as this. Space advertising in magazines is however becoming a more and more viable alternative and supplement to traditional video distribution.

Publishers

Publishers are not a market per se, but offer independent producers ideas, marketing and co-venturing opportunities. Publishers are an obvious place to look when trying to design programs for home video. Specialty programs may not find an audience in video specialty stores, but bookstores are just the place for videos based on well-known books or book genres. 1985 was a year when many publishers began to enter the video field. *Crown Publishing* produced how-tos and language tapes, and distributed classic films through their own sales force. *Knopf Video Books* released a series of *Julia Child* cooking tapes. *MacMillan Video* released *Berlitz* courses, children's programming and instructionals. *Random House Home Video* released *The Velveteen Rabbit. Reader's Digest, Scholastic Productions, Simon and Schuster* are all players as well, with specialized educational, family and children's programming. *Western Publishing* has been able to put more product into the market than anyone to date with its *Golden Books* series. How well videos will actually sell-through to the consumer from the shelf is still to be seen. A new era of video publishing has begun.

These publishers not only have clout among the book trade, but their titles and properties are well-known. Most major publishers and many smaller publishers are currently involved in developing and producing specialized videocassettes and welcome input from experienced producers and distributors. *Publishers Weekly,* the leading trade magazine, has news pieces about video almost every week. Libraries throughout the country are stocking videos. The 1986 American Booksellers Association in New Orleans saw more booths and exhibits from video suppliers and book publishers alike than ever before.

History can provide some insight as many attribute the success of the Jane Fonda video to the initial success of the book from Simon and Schuster. The book sold record numbers before the tape was produced. Later Acropolis Books produced one of the first specialty videos based on its best-selling books *Color Me Beautiful* and *The Eight-Minute Makeover*. These books found little success in the bookstores and video retail stores, but perhaps they entered the market too early. Kartes acquired the cassette rights to the books and paid Acropolis a royalty on each tape sold through bookstores and video stores. They are still selling today as backlist.

Esquire's first tape was *Ultimate Fitness*. A book was released simultaneously. The tape promoted the book and the book promoted the tape with *''bounce-back''* coupons in each.

It's no surprise that *Raquel Welch: Total Beauty and Fitness* was a success in home video. Here a coordinated campaign was designed for Raquel who toured and promoted her book and video at the same time. Both used the same cover art work. More and more video and book publishers are working together to market product. Lisa Sliwa's tape *Common Sense Defense* (Vestron) and book *Attitude* (Crown) are cross-marketed. Coordinated marketing efforts pay off for producer and author alike.

Direct Mail

Since the video retail stores place so much emphasis on *''A''* titles, direct mail may emerge as the primary method to sell-through special interest. In other similar businesses, mail order accounts for approximately 15% of revenues. It is expected that videos will reach this mark as well.

Now that VCR penetration exceeds 35%, many specialty distributors are returning to direct mail as a way to sell their specialty product to special users. It is estimated that about 5% of the business is now through mail order.

Direct response marketing was tried by several companies—*Fotomat* among them—early on in the home video business. The company lost lots of money. Most analysts agree that the reason for the failure was that there simply were not enough video machines in place to support the marketing costs involved. Also, the consumer was looking to rent tapes at low prices, not buy them at high prices through the mail. More direct response marketing campaigns used multiple ads in consumer magazines and direct mail pieces. Each ad or mail piece often reached someone without a machine—a wasted effort.

These early failures by *Time-Life, Embassy Home Video* and *3-M* had scared off many of the large companies, leaving the field open to the smaller guys who knew how to reach small but buying audiences. Many marketers are now returning. These marketers believe that when the VCR penetration hits 40%, direct marketing will make a lot of sense. Special genres, such as sports, war, collectibles and other targeted educational material sells best. Direct mail assumes that people want to collect and own tapes and that they will pay for them. This may not necessarily be true for every title, so there will undoubtedly be many failures.

Columbia House is currently a leader in the mail order business and used its record division to sell tapes. Other mail order houses are *Time's Book of the Month Club, American Express,* and *Reader's Digest.* Sharper Image sends out a catalog to its customers that promotes some video product. *Waldenbooks* also has a direct mail catalog of 300 titles that it sends to 250,000 people. The names used were all owners of VCRs. *Barnes and Noble* also mailed out a catalog with video product. The right tapes, sold to the right audience, can garner significant profits. Independent producers should pay close attention to efforts with this marketing approach and incorporate any strategies that work. Direct mail is a science.

What mail order enables the manufacturer to do is to narrow-cast a program at a narrow audience and thereby save marketing costs. Producers and manufacturers need to be careful about selecting the right titles that consumers will want to own, and keeping prices low.

Direct mail companies have gained experience selling records and books. Among them are *CBS/Columbia House, Crown Publishing, Blackhawk Films, and Reader's Digest*. At present, the main titles distributed by these direct mail companies are classics, public domain movies, instructionals, and documentaries. It is the kind of programming that mass merchandisers and video retail stores cannot afford to carry because of their limited appeal. But mail order companies can target their sales most efficiently through existing mailing lists.

Time's Book of the Month Club has taken video from an experimental stage to a point where it is now part of its service. It is offering cassettes in every mailing catalog that goes to more than 2 million members of its book club. The cassettes are sold at a low price (some as low as $9.95). The club has released *Julia Child* cooking tapes and music videos.

Reader's Digest sent a test mailing to 50,000 names around Christmas 1985 on 30 titles. By the end of 1986, it expects to be sending catalogs to more than 1 million people. It has had success with music titles such as *That's Entertainment,* but poor response with home improvement cassettes.

Publishers Central Bureau sent out a second catalog of 35 titles from Embassy Home Entertainment at $24.95. It also sells Goldwyn classics,

Ingmar Bergman features, and some 500 other public domain and feature film titles.

Other efforts include those by *Sallyforth Video* and *The Videotape Catalog,* which sell a variety of specialized tapes from many small and large producers through their catalogs. Producers of single tapes can benefit because they can reach large audiences at a low cost. Regardless of the scale, the right direct mail piece and promoting the right tape to the right audience can yield profitable returns.

Mass Merchants

Two rack jobbers, *Lieberman Enterprises* and *Handelman Company*, place video product on discount and mass merchant shelves. Examples of chains that use their services are *Target, Federated, Fedco, Sears, J.C. Penney* and *K mart*. The rack jobber is responsible for keeping the shelves or displays supplied with product. Unlike the video retail store business, the mass merchant expects to be able to return product (100% guaranteed return) if it doesn't sell. That places the manufacturer in a precarious position—he may duplicate, package and ship 50,000 cassettes, but if only 49,000 sell off the shelf and he's expected to take them back, then he's got a very serious problem.

To compound the problems of selling through mass-merchant outlets, the video manufacturer must contend with given profit margins to the rack jobber and to the mass merchant beyond the traditional margins. Furthermore, the merchants look for sell-through product priced at $29.95 or less. Sometimes much less. Return privileges and greater profit margins are the two major issues that have slowed down the process of selling videos to mass-merchant outlets. Minor problems such as selling periods that differ significantly from the weekly or biweekly video store release and order pattern are also something video manufacturers have to accommodate. Mass merchants may, for example, want selected product for special promotions throughout the year.

Children's and some specialty programs have been successful in mass-merchandiser outlets. Christmas 1985 saw titles such as Paramount's *White Christmas*, Vestron's *Mr. Mom* and *My Little Pony, Care Bears,* Spinnaker Software's educational line, Disney and others perform very well. 1985 was also the year that the penetration of video into mass-merchandise discount stores jumped from 5% to nearly 25%. Rack jobbers loaded in 120 tapes per store of about 30 to 60 titles. Videos can be successfully sold in discount stores, and one can expect these outlets to expand their commitment to video product.

SALES AND MARKETING

Sales And Marketing

"Without a massive sales and marketing effort, you might as well not release the tape."

The Retail Store

Before we explore the sales and marketing of videocassettes, let's first take a brief look at the average video rental store since it represents the core business of home video. The store has about 1,500 square feet devoted to 2,100 different titles. Within a one-mile radius there are four or five competitors. More than three-fourths of the stores are owned by men, half of whom have graduated from college. That's who's making the purchases for the consumer to rent.

The average store turns nearly a thousand transactions each week. Most of them (98%) are rentals and the rest are sales of either new or used cassettes. However, the 2% sales transactions generate approximately 21% of the store's total revenue and is rising as a percentage yearly. The combined transactions will yield approximately $3,300 per week. Revenues help the store pay the lease, staff, overhead and buy new cassettes. The average store spends about $1,000 per month on newspaper and direct mail advertising, the two most popular forms.

On the programming side, if, for example, the store is able to spend $1,100 (a third of revenue) on new cassettes, at an average price of $46, that would mean the store would be *"open-to-buy"* about 24 cassettes per week—not very many considering there are 500 new choices every month. First choice will be to buy 10 or 20 of the hot new *"A"* title like *Rambo, Ghostbusters,* or *Back to the Future*. When the rentals slow down, the store will begin to sell off these tapes to other video stores and to consumers.

It is recommended by video consultants that a video rental store mix its genres by percentage:

Comedy	15%
Action/Adventure	25%
Foreign	2%
Family	12%
Horror	11%
Martial Arts	3%
Music	3%
Classics	3%
Sports	2%
Sci-Fi	10%
How-To	3%
Westerns	6%
Adult	5%

If a retailer follows these suggestions, then he may only be open-to-buy, for example, 2.4 sci-fi films. If one of the titles he's being offered is yours, then it had better be one of the best known or it's unlikely he'll buy it. The most popular genres for the *"sell-through"* market are children's, action/adventure, how-to, music video, comedy. Adult, sci-fi, drama, horror and foreign are genres that do not sell well.

There are nearly 20 major wholesalers in the U.S. They account for nearly half of the business. (There are another 80 or so smaller wholesalers.) The largest is *Commtron*, which distributes nationwide and has approximately 21% of the market share. *Sound Video*, with approximately 5% share also distributes records. *Metro Video* works through branches, has approximately 5% market share, and sells to the more densely populated areas on the East and West coasts. One of the fastest-growing wholesalers is *Ingram*, which distributes videos to specialty outlets and bookstores. These wholesalers solicit their network of video dealers and then place orders to the manufacturers.

Here are the mechanics of distribution. Videotapes are sold to the video retailers by wholesalers (also called distributors). Wholesalers are middlemen who work between the retailer and the video manufacturer. They receive margins of 10%-12%, but as competition increases, they often cut their margins to 7% or 8%. They usually receive 30 to 60 days credit, while the retailers need 60 to 90 days in order to recoup their investment through rentals. Some major manufacturers sell directly to the larger retail stores, thereby going around the wholesaler. It's already tough for the wholesaler because he may sell to the same retail stores as his competition. To make a sale, he may need to discount the product and take an even smaller profit margin.

Marketing

Marketing is creating a consumer need and then filling it through a particular video program. The creator or acquirer of programs (the program supplier or manufacturer) markets its videos to wholesalers with special promotions and sale incentives, trade and consumer press coverage, advertising in consumer and trade magazines, point-of-purchase materials, through video trailers and coming-soon reels, posters, banners and other giveaways. The marketing campaign will address the consumer need and convince the wholesaler that this is a program that the video retailer will want because the consumer will want it. It's a three-step process with all participants along the way (manufacturer, wholesaler, retailer) taking a shot at what they think consumers will want to rent or buy.

The manufacturer's marketing arm will make regular calls to wholesalers, retailers and duplicators to identify new trends and opportunities. Regular visits to dealers help refine the selling process, develop closer relationships and solve logistical distribution problems. Through this interaction, a manufacturer gains a clearer idea about how to sell his product. Obviously, the more promotional support that a manufacturer can provide the wholesaler, the better job the wholesaler can do. Some program suppliers or manufacturers also send posters and one-sheets to the network of dealers, even though they do not sell directly to the dealers. (These are particularly important because three-fourths of all sales are made by telephone. Good printed material sells cassettes.) This increases the video retailer's awareness of the programs that are about to be released. When the wholesaler comes to make the sale, the retailer is already aware of it. At the same time, there are promotions to consumers in the hope that they will go to the video store and ask for the tape. This helps *"pull it through."*

It is very expensive and time-intensive to promote programs. This is especially true when there are literally hundreds of individual programs bidding for attention each and every month from dozens of program suppliers.

It is the program supplier's job to stay in touch with both the wholesalers and the dealers, to try and identify new opportunities in the marketplace, and to promote existing programs. Manufacturers and wholesalers are watching one another to determine trends in the market, what their competitors are spending, how their sales programs are structured and how to improve their own sales. There is fierce competition for both wholesaler and retailer attention and shelf space.

Because the traditional video market is a two-tiered selling arena, it is a complex and challenging process. Those who succeed have done so because they have efficiently used all the marketing and promotional tools available. For an individual program to succeed, the manufacturer and wholesaler must get behind it, pulling out every marketing stop. Without a massive effort, one might as well forget releasing a tape at all—it just won't perform.

Each year the *Video Software Dealers Association (VSDA)* meets. Thousands of dealers come together for this video trade convention. In

1985 it was entitled *"Sellabration."* The event consists of each of the larger program suppliers courting the distributors (wholesalers) and retailers, holding parties and luncheons and promoting new programs.

There are also sessions where the business as a whole is discussed. One of the major issues that was discussed in 1985 from the point of view of the retailers was price protection. Their concerns were with a technique that program suppliers have of selling a program at a high price initially and then lowering the price several months later. They feel that if program suppliers lower the price that they too will wait to buy. (Price protection means that if the price is later reduced, the retailer gets a refund or credit if he bought at the higher price.) Retailers are also concerned that there are too many people into the retail business and that there is no more expansion of the dealer base. Also, video retailers are threatened by mass merchants who, because of volume, are able to purchase programs at lower prices, thus squeezing the traditional video retailer out. The distributors (wholesalers) are caught in the middle and are most worried about the program suppliers selling direct to the larger video retail chains. On the other hand, the program suppliers are looking for every possibility to expand direct sales to larger retail accounts. They also expect better service from their distributors over their competitors. As in any business, they are looking to expand distribution, and mass merchants, bookstores and others are a bright light in their future.

There is now a glut of new product in the marketplace—so much so that retailers simply cannot absorb it. Many expect that this overcompetition will cause the number of video retail stores to diminish. They are wary that beginning in 1986 there will be a big shakeout in the video industry at all levels. Among retailers there are simply too many players who are undercapitalized and have little marketing experience. Many will find it difficult to survive.

Each of the 20,000 to 25,000 video stores now in existence has about 2,500 to 3,000 titles. The stores charge an average of $3 per night for rentals. To stay in business they need 1,000 steady customers. With so many stores competing for the same business, the number of customers and rentals is reduced. Furthermore, a store must obtain new programs at the same time as its competition or it will lose customers. Therefore, the store is almost forced to buy multiple copies of "*A*" titles.

Video retailers fear the pressure from highly competitive experienced mass merchants who buy product in volume. MGM's Cy Leslie thinks that mass merchants currently hold 5% of the business. He expects this to increase to 15%-20% by late 1986. Will consumers begin to wander away from rentals when they can buy tapes at low cost from mass merchandisers? The next years will answer this question.

The video business is a business in flux. There will be many changes in the years to come. The changing marketplace should be monitored by producers because the economics will impact how and where their programs will be sold and rented.

Marketing Tools

Program suppliers use a variety of marketing tools to promote their programs to both wholesalers and retailers. These materials are essential to the selling process. (Producers can participate by pre-designing these marketing tools prior to or at the same time that they are developing their programs. The distributor may or may not use the suggested approach if a better angle is found, but it will greatly assist the producer in creating the content of the show and exploring the program's potential.) It is important to remember that a wholesaler and retailer will make a purchasing decision based on the marketing tools he sees—long before the program is on the shelf.

The one-sheet is one or more pages that sell the program. It has a primary graphic that is also used on the box. The copy lines highlight the promotable elements of the program.

Ad mats are screened line art that the wholesaler and retailer can use for their own ads. They give this to their local newpaper that inserts the store's name and address and other particulars.

Giveaways or *''chachkis''* are merchandise premiums like key chains, glasses, pads, pens or other clever gimmicks that correspond to the program. They are given to the wholesalers and retailers. These help to remind them that the program is on the way. Father Guido Sarducci's giveaway was a priest collar with the title of the tape. *Richard Pryor: Live and Smokin'* was promoted with a cigarette lighter with the title emblazoned on the side. *National Geographic Video* was promoted with a free subscription to National Geographic magazine.

The program supplier or manufacturer will mail packets of these and other materials to their wholesalers. Some program suppliers will send a mailing to each and every retail outlet in the country. This mailing will include a letter and a one-sheet relating to the title and other *''coming soon''* material.

The program supplier also sends letters and posters to the wholesaler's sales reps who sell through telemarketing or road calls.

The retailers also receive P-O-P (point-of-purchase) material. These range from giveaways to merchandising aids such as posters, banners, mobiles, order forms and large stand-up displays.

Trailers ranging in length from 30 to 90 seconds are compilations of various scenes from the program—much like a movie coming attraction. The wholesalers can sample the tapes so they know what they are being asked to sell.

Space advertisements promote individual programs or groups of programs in trade magazines such as *Video Store, Video Insider, Video Business, Billboard* and appropriate consumer magazines. The manufacturer or program supplier is responsible for preparing, placing and paying for the various ads that announce the program. The cost of designing ads, placing them, and launching mail campaigns is very significant. And this is only a sampling of what program suppliers will do to promote a title. It is a very complex and expensive process.

It would be worthwhile for producers to visit their local video stores and look at some of the material that program suppliers and distributors have sent, and while doing so, imagine what some of the materials for their own programs may look like. Talk to retailers about the most effective marketing tools that they have. Go to school on what's been done that has worked.

PACKAGING

Packaging

"A good package will stop 'em in their tracks."

Packaging

Marketing relies on a well-designed package. A good package will stop 'em in their tracks. With literally hundreds of tapes coming out each month, the importance is underlined. The package design may also be used on one-sheets and other promotional materials. It should immediately bring forth an image—an expectation of what the program is about. The content, flavor and promotable elements of a program will in three or four seconds imprint themselves upon the viewer's mind—and hopefully he will decide to buy or rent the tape.

What follows are examples of packaging where I have some involvement and where I have some insight into why something was done a certain way. Some were more successful than others. Each package can be analyzed and evaluated on whether it succeeds or not in selling the program.

Hardware Wars. Hardware Wars, a parody of *"Star Wars,"* is a popular and successful short film that I produced in the late '70s. It was one of the first independent shorts to be released in home video in 1982—long before there was much of a market. It has seen cumulative sales of about 5,000 to 6,000 units. When Warner Home Video first began designing packages for its home videos, it created a generic orange and black format for its boxes—to distinguish them from competing product. The company no longer does this. And rightfully so—it's not appropriate for every title. After all, no one really cares if a program is on Warner or Vestron or RCA. What consumers are interested in is the program itself.

The Hardware Wars short film is compiled with other short films: in this case *Bambi Meets Godzilla, Closet Cases of the Nerd Kind,* and *Porklips Now. Hardware Wars* was the best-known title and therefore was used as the key element on the package.

The box itself is somewhat cluttered, yet the main impression—that this is a sci-fi comedy—comes through. The Hardware Wars type on the poster is similar to Star Wars typography as are the elements of the poster. The line *''May The Farce Be With You''* is also a tip that it's a comedy. The package's weakness is that it is a bit cluttered, but then again the audience of 12-year-olds likes to study the package as they would a cereal box; in that respect it works. Had Warner decided not to do a generic box, there would be more space for a larger title and graphics. The package design should be pushed to resemble a motion picture even more, and the title Hardware Wars need not be duplicated at the top of the border. Nevertheless, I'd give this a B+ in terms of design, execution and promotion of the program.

Academy Award Winners. The program is a compilation of Academy Award-winning animated short films. Overall the package design is very weak. The fact that these are *''winners''* is lost. It looks like a kid's program. There is too much type. However, the contract required that all the titles and filmmakers' names be on the front cover. A better title and package design might have used the Academy's gold *Oscar* or a facsimile. Unfortunately, it is a trademarked character and the *Motion Picture Academy of Arts and Sciences* will not allow us its commercial use, even though each film included in the compilation won an Academy Award. Had the package included the statuette—which is immediately recognizable—it would have signaled to the viewer that this was an award-winning package. The typeface and red packaging both help to make the program jump off the shelf but it takes a minute to know what the program is about. Rating: C-.

WARNER HOME VIDEO
COMEDY
Hardware Wars and Other Film Farces
HARDWARE WARS
FLUKE
THE FARCE WITH YOU
"HARDWARE WARS"
"BAMBI MEETS GODZILLA"
"CLOSET CASES OF THE NERD KIND"
"PORKLIPS NOW"
VHS

ACADEMY
AWARD
WINNERS
ANIMATED
SHORT FILMS
ACADEMY AWARD WINNERS ANIMATED SHORT FILMS
Compiled and coordinated by DEAN BERKO
Awarded 1983—Jimmy Picker's SUNDAE IN NEW YORK
Directed by Jimmy Picker
Awarded 1981—CRAC! Directed by Fredric Back
Awarded 1960—Jules Feiffer's MUNRO
Directed by Gene Deitch
Awarded 1962—THE HOLE Awarded 1959 MOONBIRD
both Directed by John & Faith Hubley
Awarded 1974—CLOSED MONDAYS Directed by Will Vinton
& Bob Gardiner

Comedy Videos. This is a compilation of comedy videos by top comics and music acts. This package has the same difficulties as the previous two—the content of the show is not immediately clear. It is compounded because of the compilation nature of the show. Here the most recognizable names—*Mel Brooks, Martin Mull, The Blues Brothers*. Others were also promoted. Unfortunately—for my money—the names get equal billing and the pictures are too small in relation to the names. As a Monday morning quarterback, I think it might have been packaged better by utilizing a few of the big names with strong graphics and simply listing the lesser names in a smaller typeface. The copy line *"They're weird. They're wild. They're Comedy Videos."* is good but it gets lost in the typography. The title Comedy Videos is strong and sold a reasonable number of cassettes. Rating: C.

Lords of the Ring. A clever title for this wrestling compilation featuring matches with Rick Flair, Jerry Lawler, Dusty Rhodes and others. The collage on the cover conveys excitement and clearly shows that there's a lot in this program. The art work speaks directly to the target audience—via its blood red cover, action-packed, outrageous wrestlers, music by George Thorogood, etc. The tape sold well. There was no question what the tape was about. Rating: A.

Joe Piscopo. This show is a one-hour special. There are a variety of skits with Joe doing his best characterizations. The packaging succeeds because first, it promotes Joe Piscopo, and secondly, it uses Joe's various impersonations—*David Letterman, Jerry Lewis* and *Joan Rivers*—on the cover. The graphics and photos are very striking. The photos are cleverly wrapped around the entire box—a unique approach. The box even looks good displayed spine-out and features a picture of Joe as *Andy Rooney*. It's fun to look at the box—everyone's Joe Piscopo! The hook-line, *"You've seen him on Saturday Night Live, but not all of him . . . and never like this!"* promises something more. The show delivers. Eddie Murphy's name could be more prominently displayed on the box; however, this is a small point. The packaging is very classy with its light gray background. Rating: A+.

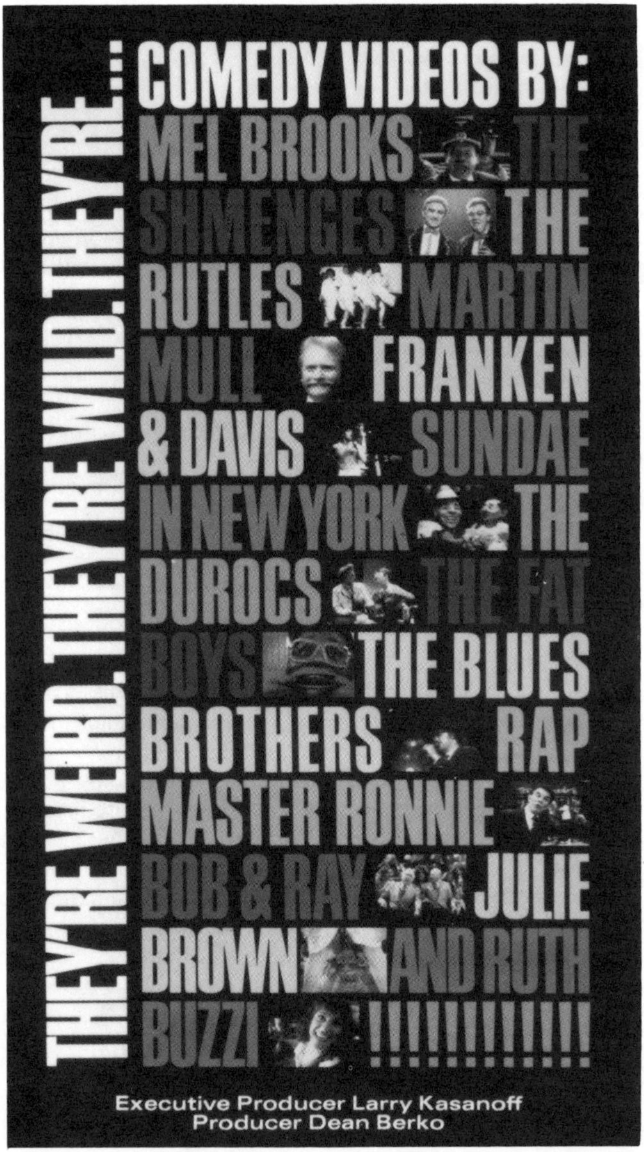
THEY'RE WEIRD. THEY'RE WILD. THEY'RE...
COMEDY VIDEOS BY:
MEL BROOKS THE
SHMENGES THE
RUTLES MARTIN
MULL FRANKEN
& DAVIS SUNDAE
IN NEW YORK THE
DUROCS THE FAT
BOYS THE BLUES
BROTHERS RAP
MASTER RONNIE
BOB & RAY JULIE
BROWN AND RUTH
BUZZI !!!!!!!!!!!!
Executive Producer Larry Kasanoff
Producer Dean Berko

THE
ROAD WARRIORS,
"NATURE BOY" RIC FLAIR,
JERRY "THE KING" LAWLER,
DUSTY RHODES,
"ROWDY" RODDY PIPER,
GORGEOUS GEORGE
AND MUCH MUCH MORE!
PRESENTS
LORDS OF THE RING
SUPERSTARS
AND
SUPERBOUTS
MUSIC BY
GEORGE
THOROGOOD
AND THE
DESTROYERS

JOE
The
PISCOPO
Video
Joe Piscopo.
You've Seen Him On "Saturday Night Live."
But Not All of Him...And Never Like This!
With Special Guest EDDIE MURPHY

Truly Tasteless Jokes
THE VIDEO
Based on the best-selling books compiled by
Blanche Knott
Produced and Directed by Peter Robert

Truly Tasteless Jokes. This is a comedy tape featuring eight stand-up comics (that no one has ever heard of). They tell truly tasteless jokes—the show delivers on your expectations. The packaging is exactly like the book—same typeface, same yellow cover as the best-selling book. There is no doubt what the show is. *"You liked the book, you'll love the video"* is the copy line. Package rating: A+.

National Geographic. The programs are the high-quality National Geographic specials as seen on PBS. The package design duplicates the magazine's typography and yellow border. It looks like something you'd want to own. It looks *"collectible."* The graphics and key photograph are strong. The package needs no copy to sell it. You know what to expect. Rating: A+.

Weight Watchers Magazine: Guide to a Healthy Lifestyle. This package also communicates exactly what the program is. The familiar *Weight Watchers* trademark name and pink packaging is consistent with *Weight Watchers Magazine*, the best-selling books, and the frozen foods. The colors appeal to women, the primary audience. *Lynn Redgrave* is well-known, and as a host, brings credibility to the program. Many people know that she lost a great deal of weight. She is also the spokesperson for Weight Watchers and has been seen on television in their commercials. The tape measure on the package informs us that the tape is about losing weight. Rating: A+.

Hooker. This is a hard-hitting documentary. The show itself is a *"talking heads"*-style interview with prostitutes and call girls. Because documentaries are not the most popular home video form and movies are, the program is sold more like a movie. The key art is reminiscent of the top-grossing film *"Angel."* The title itself is lean and descriptive, and packs a wallop when combined with the artist's rendering. Again, right away, you know what to expect. Package design rating: A+.

Best Legs in the Eighth Grade. This is a comedy special that was seen on HBO. This tape was only exposed on HBO and sold very well when

NATIONAL
GEOGRAPHIC
VIDEO
LAND
OF THE TIGER
Enter the world of
the exquisite jungle cat.

WEIGHT WATCHERS®
MAGAZINE
Guide To A Healthy Lifestyle
Hosted By
Lynn Redgrave
Photographed by Christopher Little/ABC
Executive Producer Lawrence Kasanoff

Hooker
"...a remarkable achievement—frank and open-minded, and troubling."
—CableVision
This bold and informative look at life on the streets brings the harsh realities of the "world's oldest profession" to the screen. A film of immense power, HOOKER answers the questions that were, until now, too intimate to ask.
This vivid and disturbing film paints a painfully clear portrait of three types of female prostitutes: call girls, girls who work at nude "modeling" parlors and street walkers. HOOKER offers a rare and personal glimpse of these prostitutes during their public times and private moments; as they describe encounters with their tricks, their pimps, their lovers, and the law.
Hailed as a "remarkable achievement," and "an unblinking and unsensationalized view, full of vivid, haunting faces and startling remarks," this American Film Festival Award winner uncovers a way of life rarely seen by "outsiders."
VHS: VA3104; Beta: VB3104; 79 Minutes.
Creative Marketing Company of the Year (as voted by the readers of VIDEO INSIDER)
VESTRON VIDEO
© 1985 Vestron Video P.O. Box 4000 Stamford, CT 06907

TIM
MATHESON
JIM
BELUSHI
ANNETTE
O'TOOLE
The
BEST LEGS
in the 8TH
GRADE
THEY WERE SEXY BACK THEN.
NOW THEY'RE IRRESISTIBLE!

distributed by Lightning Video. The graphics themselves are particularly strong, the title is catchy, and stars such as Jim Belushi help. The hook-line, *"They were sexy back then, now they're irresistible!"* is well-conceived and catchy. It works! Packaging design: A.

When setting out to have your cover designed, it's important to design art that speaks to your target audience. Do not try to win art director awards or to use the last crayon painting that your genius kid did. The more suited the cover is to your audience's tastes, the more successful the program will be.

Producers and designers of home video packages should always ask themselves: What are the key promotable elements in the program? What is the genre? How can it be communicated graphically? What colors, type and design elements can make the package stand out from the others? What well-known names appear that can lend recognition value to the tape? What trademarks, book titles or previously exposed design elements can be utilized? It is important that the package be designed so that it communicates *"what it is"* in just a few brief seconds. The more attractive (and appropriate) the packaging, the quicker it will get into the hands of consumers. As much care should go into the packaging as went into the program. Remember, a retailer or potential purchaser will see the package before the program. If they don't like it, they'll never get to the program.

PRESS AND PUBLICITY

Press And Publicity

"Publicity differs from advertising—you don't have to pay for it."

Press and Publicity

Once the program has been completed, a new phase of work begins. Without a tremendous push through press and publicity no tape will find an audience. People need to hear about the tape through all forms of media—local and national television, radio, newspapers and magazines.

Producers and publicists can sit down together and design an extensive media campaign that will reach the target audience. Publicity differs from advertising—you don't have to pay for it. But you must find an angle that will interest the media so your story will be told. There are many levels and many ways that a videotape can be promoted. The producer does not want to overlook any promotional opportunity—it all pays off.

First, promote the program to the video trade—the wholesaler and the video retailer. The trade learns about the program through marketing tools sent to them six to eight weeks before the videotape is released. They are primed for the program so that by order time they are pre-disposed to want to buy it. Hopefully, they've allotted some money for such a purchase. They can be reached through trade publications, such as *Video Marketing* and *Video Insider*. A press kit can be prepared that exploits every promotable angle. If there is a star, this promotable element should lead the promotion. An engaging and appealing synopsis of the program can be written. Quotes can be extracted from the producer, director, and other participants. Black and white and color photos can accompany the press kit, along with a "*coming soon*" trailer of the program. A music video, if appropriate, can also be edited.

Consumers too need to hear about the tape. Hopefully, they'll ask to rent it at their local store. Or perhaps they'll go to their bookstore to buy it. A reel of clips from the program can be assembled and sent to the major television programs that may be interested. *Entertainment Tonight, Good Morning America,* the *Today Show, Johnny Carson, David Letterman,* and others are the top national shows for promotion. Do not begin your promotion until the tapes are actually available. No sense in starting too soon. You'll only get one shot at it. And timing is everything.

If there is a recognizable star in the program, enlist his or her aid in promoting it. Stars stand a better chance at guest appearances than unknowns. They can appear on talk shows, be interviewed by newspapers, magazines, television and radio. They can even make in-store appearances. The more a star promotes the tape, the better it will do. If there is a book of the same title or a record album that has just come out featuring the same artists, the video company, record company, publisher and star can join together to promote all products simultaneously.

Send copies of the program to consumer video magazines and major newspapers for review. Send them well in advance of the release because many publications have extremely long lead times. If favorable reviews are obtained in advance of the release of the tape, excerpts can be used on one-sheets, packaging and in follow-up promotional material.

Sometimes a program is made for another medium before it reaches home video. A program may play theatrically or on pay television before it reaches home video. In this case, because of the sequencing, there are three distinct opportunities to promote the tape. Take advantage of each.

There are many other things that publicists will come up with to assist in the promotion. A launch party? A premiere? Special promotions in different cities? A multitown celebrity tour? A benefit opening? A press luncheon? All efforts are to achieve free publicity in addition to the paid advertising that must be bought for the program. The tape will receive most of its attention when it is first released. But it will be difficult to keep the program *"alive"* in the public's mind without continued publicity.

Major distributors have their own publicity and promotion departments, or they hire outside publicists. Producers can meet with the distributor's press department and brainstorm publicity ideas. The more defined and well organized the publicity campaign, the better the result.

INCOME PROJECTIONS

Income Projections

"Design and sell your programs to a variety of markets."

Income Projections

Producers who make a living producing do so because they are able to design and sell their programs to a variety of markets. It is unlikely that any one market can provide enough income to pay for production costs let alone generate profit. If you don't think about as many markets as possible when you are designing your project, it will be all the more difficult to sell it later on. If you've already made some inroads to distribution outlets early on, you maximize your program's ability to pay off.

What follows are income projections for a fictional program entitled *"Couch Potato Marathon."* And believe me, it really is fiction. The income projection table is meant to serve as a guide in determining how to sequence and release your program in various markets. Use the format if you like, but do not use these numbers for your own project. They are made up and not representational of anything. This is a fantasy. If you use these numbers and lose your shirt, it's your problem. Better that you research each market yourself as it pertains to your specific program. Then your income projections may mean something and be useful to you.

The income projection table covers three years from the initial release. Displayed are the gross revenues earned by the program, the percentage of gross returned to the producer, and the net receipts.

Our fictitious program is *The Couch Potato Marathon,* a 90-minute,

16mm program where top stars participate in the thrilling event. The budget is $175,000. The stars bring marketability to the program in a variety of markets.

"COUCH POTATO MARATHON"
INCOME PROJECTIONS

MARKETS	1987	1988	1989	GROSS	PROD %	NET
SPONSOR	25,000			25,000	1	25,000
THEATRICAL	200,000			200,000	.125	25,000
FOREIGN THEATRICAL	0			0	0	0
PAY TV	75,000			75,000	1	75,000
HOME VIDEO		400,000	100,000	500,000	.15	75,000
BUSINESS/INDUSTRY		50,000		50,000	.25	12,500
PSA		50,000		50,000	1	50,000
PREMIUMS		120,000		120,000	.15	18,000
FOREIGN HOME VIDEO		10,000		10,000	1	10,000
SYNDICATION			25,000	25,000	.7	17,500
FOREIGN TV			5,000	5,000	.6	3,000
						311,000
					BUDGET	175,000
					PROFIT $	136,000

Here is an explanation of how the income flows from various markets.

Sponsor. The producer is clever. He got a sponsor, *Big Boy Potato Chips*, to put up $25,000, which he uses for the production. In exchange the sponsor gets the franchise to sell potato chips to the audience, and the chips bags are seen in the hands of fans in the bleachers. The company also gets to hang large banners along the playing field. In this case 100% of revenues are passed through to the producer because he makes this deal himself without any middlemen.

Theatrical. The producer finds a theatrical distributor to release the film in a limited manner in the U.S. The test screenings prove that like "*The Gods Must Be Crazy,*" there is an audience for this quirky film. For a film of this kind, it does very well, and box office grosses are $200,000. The distributor makes a very good deal and collects 50% or $100,000 from the exhibitor. From this amount he subtracts print and advertising costs of $50,000. The balance is shared 50/50 with the producer who receives $25,000. (He ends up receiving 12.5% of the gross.)

Foreign Theatrical. Foreign markets can make no sense of this program, so there are no foreign theatrical sales.

Pay TV. This filmed event looks pretty good to HBO or Showtime, mainly because of the stars. They pay $75,000 to license the program. The successful theatrical release, good reviews and cult following helped and they thought it would work well for late night audiences. The producer made the deal himself so no fees are deducted.

Home Video. The program sells for $29 ($20 wholesale) and sells 20,000 units—a big hit! Gross revenues are $400,000; the producer's share is $60,000, which he was paid as an advance. The next year the video grosses $100,000 and his share is $15,000. Total revenues from home video are $75,000.

Business and Industry. Remarkably enough, the producers are able to re-edit a business and industry one-hour program, which is motivational and instructional in nature. The producer also designs a workbook and audiotapes to accompany a video. The whole packet sells for $500. This is the training/motivational package that the corporations have been waiting for to inspire their sales staff to better performance. One hundred programs are sold and net the distributor $50,000. The producer receives a 25% royalty of $12,500. (Now it's highly unlikely that most shows could be designed for entertainment and business and industry markets, but it's thrown in here as an example of an auxillary exploitable market. Only a few programs will really be appropriate for this market.)

PSA. There are 10 major stars that appear in the *Couch Potato Marathon*. During the shoot, the producer cleverly produces a package of one-minute public service announcements. Each star talks about the virtues of staying in school. Ten sponsors contribute $5,000 each. The PSAs are sent free to television stations.

Premiums. The potato chip manufacturer, *Big Boy Potato Chips*, is so pleased with how the tape comes out it decides to run a national contest where 10,000 winners will receive a videocassette of the event. Cassettes are ordered for a special price of $12 each from the manufacturer for a total gross of $120,000; the producer's 15% share is $24,000.

Foreign Home Video. Many of the stars in the show are popular in Japan so the home video rights are licensed for an advance of $10,000. Unfortunately, not enough sales are made so the advance is never recouped and no further royalties are paid.

Syndication. In the third year following its release, the television syndicators pick up this one-time special for $25,000. The distributor keeps 30%, and 70%, or $17,500, is returned to the producer.

Foreign TV. An international television distributor takes on the program and sells it in a few small markets. Gross receipts are $5,000. The producer's share is 60% of $3,000.

Net Profit. The production budget of $175,000 is deducted from the accumulated gross over the three years. The net profit to the producer is $136,000. The producer was able to maximize revenues by selling off the rights in a variety of markets. The sequencing was designed so that each sale was made to each market giving it enough time protection to be fully exploited. The producer also designed a film that would have as many markets as possible.

In this imaginary scenario things worked out remarkably well and the producer received a fairly standard royalty from all markets. If the film is desirable to many distributors, perhaps the producer could negotiate higher royalties. In any case, this income projection chart demonstrates the variety of markets and income that can be derived from a film over a three-year period of time. Your project many differ significantly from this hypothetical model. Research among distributors in the various markets will give you a better sense of what your program will be worth and how much you can expect to receive for it.

THE FUTURE

The Future

"Producers who are creative, studious, and imaginative will come up with tomorrow's megahits."

Future Issues

The video industry is still in its infancy although it is moving toward maturity. With this transition, the business is changing at a tremendous rate. New issues arise each month, and programmers, manufacturers, wholesalers and retailers alike must find ways to cope with these changes, with new opportunities and challenges. Among the problems and great possibilities on the horizon are:

Tape Piracy. It's anybody's guess how deeply piracy cuts into home video revenues: 1%, 10%, 25%. In order to curb the expansion of piracy (the unauthorized distribution and sale of copyrighted material), manufacturers have utilized anti-piracy devices (such as *Macrovision*) so that tapes cannot be copied. The device is expensive (10 to 35 cents per copy), and there is no real indication that any more tapes are sold because they cannot be duplicated. Nevertheless, these and other systems will be used in the future by manufacturers.

Used Tape. A dirty word among distributors. Since retailers often overbuy "*A*" titles when there is a great demand, and sell them off only a few weeks later, a secondary "*used tape*" market has developed. These second-hand tape dealers then sell the tapes to new stores that are opening (thus depriving manufacturers of selling new tapes to these stores at normal prices). What retailers may fail to understand is that by selling off their used tapes, they are allowing other retailers to enter the business at low cost, and thus, ultimately, they are supporting their own competitors! Used tape sales cut down the volume of orders that would normally go to the original manufacturers.

Title Glut. Over 500 titles are released each month. Because the retailer spends most of his money on the *''A''* titles, there is little left over for the *''B''*, *''C''*, and *''D''* title. Sales of the lesser titles are falling off greatly as stores become well stocked and hit-driven. Many feel it will become more and more difficult for manufacturers to sell lesser programming to the rental trade.

Rights Costs. Because the business is turning toward the popular, easy-to-rent hits and because of the limited number of *''A''* titles, manufacturers are combating in fierce bidding wars for these titles with prices escalating to $5 million and $6 million per picture. Independents like Vestron have entered the motion picture business and will finance and produce their own feature films, thus obtaining not only worldwide home video rights, but theatrical and television rights as well.

The Big Shakeout. Since most video specialty stores rent—not sell—tapes, a second video business, the sell-through market has developed. Now mass merchandisers and other volume retail chains are able to buy tapes at low prices to compete with the *''mom and pop shops.''* In addition, with the tremendous glut of product available, the video retailer cannot begin to buy it all. Even so, once a consumer has seen all the titles in his shop, he moves on to other stores with different inventory. Thus, the retailer loses what was once a loyal customer. Furthermore, because the smaller video stores are undercapitalized and there is greater and greater competition for the same consumers, a shakeout is expected to occur within the next two years. It's a brave new world; not everyone will make it.

The number of video rental stores is expected to fall about 30%-40% in the next five years. When an industry moves from the early stages of a product's life into a more mature market where the most potential buyers have already purchased a VCR, there is no new market and competitors begin slashing prices. At the same time alternative sell-through markets are expanding at a tremendous rate. Furthermore, some say that the desire to rent falls off after about a year. When fewer new VCR owners enter the marketplace, who will the video stores rent tapes to? Or will prices be so low that people will want to own tapes?

Distribution Outlets. Ownership seems to be the wave of the future. As many as four times as much revenue will be generated by mass merchants selling sell-through product as against video stores renting. Bookstores will increase their revenues more than three times, and drug/convenience stores will expand twofold in the next few years. Toy stores will explode with new low-price sell-through product. Direct mail, because of high VCR penetration, will finally be feasible and revenues will increase five times.

Sell-Through. Since the VCR machine base is increasing, there is a greater opportunity than ever before to create tremendous sales volume on priced-to-sell titles. The producers of films do not participate in rental income; therefore, manufacturers feel they can reap greater profits by selling tapes at low prices (less than $29). The video retailer, who is basically in the rental business, now has competitors among mass merchant, bookstore and record store outlets who sell tapes. If the video retailer wants to hold onto his consumers, he too will have to learn how to sell as well as rent tapes.

Pay-Per-View. Just as home video has begun to establish distribution channels, a new technology—pay-per-view—comes along. Pay-per-view is frequently touted as the greatest threat to the home video because it can deliver programming directly to the home on demand. A viewer is charged automatically for every program he or she views through an addressable cable box, much like hotels do today. There are six companies that have either entered or are about to enter the pay-per-view business. Proponents of pay-per-view are trying to create a release window before, or at least at the same time as, home video, thus cutting out many viewers who may otherwise obtain their programming on videocassette.

The optimists, who favor home video, say that the cost of equipping homes with addressable boxes is a slow process at best, given cable TV's current down-trend. They believe that it would be difficult to get a viewer to pay for individual programs since they are now getting an entire monthly program service for one fee. The changeover could be met with great resistance. Large-scale pay-per-view operations may still be years away but this is an issue of concern to the entire video industry and is closely watched. Even today there are 9 million homes with addressable boxes. Is a new distribution system looming?

Optimistic Scenarios

Nevertheless, there are optimistic visionaries like David Wilkofsky and Arthur Gruen of Wilkofsky Gruen Associates, an independent business analyst. They recently published a report on the video industry, which was commissioned by Merrill Lynch and projects a booming business over the next decade. Some of their findings suggest that:

Home video will generate $20 billion in annual revenue in 1995. This is based on 4 billion rentals, and 700 million sales. VCRs will have an 85% penetration rate. VCR purchases will mirror the growth curve of color television sets.

Merrill Lynch, who also conducted market research, is more conservative. Its research points to major shakeouts among the retail outlets, independent distributors and a decline in prices for prerecorded cassettes. It also expects the prices of production and acquisition to rise, and for hardware sales to flatten and maybe even diminish. It predicts price cutting at the wholesale and retail levels, and increased return policies.

Merrill-Lynch points to the increase in sell-through revenues. Some suggest the percentages to be equal before 1990.

Retail Sales to Rentals

	Sales	Rentals
1983	19%	81%
1984	26%	74%
1985	28%	72%

Source: Merrill-Lynch

Hardware. The Wilkofsky-Gruen report says that hardware will reach 85% of TV households and that VCR penetration and growth will mirror the comparable growth of color television sales; VCRs will grow at a faster rate because the VCR is cheaper, households are more affluent, and the VCR is more versatile. The 8mm format, small, compact and portable, may become the second machine for family households as it becomes the new home movie medium.

Software Rentals. Software rentals will reach 4 billion, sales will reach 700 million units, and prerecorded cassettes will be 850 million units. Twenty billion dollars will be spent on renting and purchasing cassettes by 1990. Unlike some doomsayers, the Wilkofsky report says that new VCR purchasers are using prerecorded cassettes more than long-time VCR owners. They've got the habit and know that their machines can be used for far more than time-shifting. A Nielsen survey indicates that rental activity is on the increase. In 1984 about 37% of VCR owners rented tapes; in 1985 that increased to about 45%. The average number of tapes rented per month per VCR owner grew from 5.3 in 1984 to 6.3 in 1985. On a yearly basis (calculating for all VCR owners, even those who don't rent), the average household rented 24 tapes in 1984 and 34 in 1985. New VCR owners rented 46 tapes in 1984 and 55 in 1985. This increase in the use of prerecorded cassettes by VCR owners suggests that the home video revolution is more than a fad.

Market Size. Distributors will generate $13 billion in cassette sales. Should manufacturers embrace a low-price strategy so that cassettes can compete in price with hardcover books or records of less than $15, then shipments may increase to 1.8 billion units and $18 billion in sales. This would cause rentals to fall to 2 billion transactions from 4 billion and sales to increase 1.7 billion from 700 million at the video retail level.

Second machines (and replacement machines—they last only five years or less) will be sold in greater numbers in 1987-88, boosting sales to new levels (beyond the current three-year plateau of 10-12 million) to 14 million, then 24 million by 1995.

Video Revenues in Movie-Making. The report projects the strength of the home video market in revenue share among the other media markets.

Film Producer Revenues

	1985		1995	
Revenue Source	**($Bil)**	**Share**	**($Bil)**	**Share**
Domestic	$4.5	68%	$ 14.0	70%
Box Office	1.7	26	2.7	14
Television	.4	6	.2	1
Pay TV	.8	12	1.1	6
Cassette	1.6	24	10.0	50
Foreign	2.1	32	6.0	30
Box Office	1.0	15	2.2	11
All Television	.2	3	.8	4
Cassette	.9	14	3.0	15
Total	$ 6.6	100%	$ 20.0	100%

Source: Wilkofsky-Gruen

Programming Mix. This too will change. According to the Gallup Reports for 1985 and the Wilkofsky report for 1995, programming genres will shift. This is good news for the producers of original programming. In fact, in the future, feature films will represent far less than half of all programming.

	1985	1995	Change
Theatrical	50%	30%	−20%
Children	20%	30%	+10%
Music	15%	20%	+ 5%
Other	15%	20%	+ 5%

This and other information indicate that if producers anticipate these programming changes in the marketplace and if they position themselves as producers of children's, music or alternative programming, they may well have full production slates by 1995!

Furthermore, book publishers, record companies, computer software and educational producers and sponsors are all looking to expand into home video. The home video appetite easily outstrips Hollywood's ability to produce enough films, so that original home video programming production will be undertaken by every manufacturer, thereby increasing opportunities for independents in the next few years.

Producers will have to be cautious. Home video is a changing and transient marketplace. One cannot be a pessimist nor an optimist carried away by these future projections. There will be tremendous competition from major and minor players alike. Production budgets will have to be realistic. Many original programs will fail. Nevertheless, producers who are creative, studious, and imaginative will come up with tomorrow's megahits. *I hope you are one of them.*

APPENDIX

VIDEO DISTRIBUTORS

Video Distributors

The following lists are distributors who produce, acquire and manufacture home video programs. Some are subsidiaries of major motion picture companies; others are independents. Some are non-theatrical video distributors who sell to hospitals, universities, government, business and industry.

This list includes the primary contacts and distributors' specialties. Since this is a highly transient industry, new people may have filled these positions when you call or write. This list should give you a good start. Happy hunting.

ABC VIDEO ENTERPRISES, 2040 Avenue of the Stars, Los Angeles, CA 90067, (213) 557-6600. Herb Granath, president; Marvinia Hunter, aquisition and development of original programs. Distributes recent features, how-to, sports, cultural, children's, science, entertainment.

ACTIVE HOME VIDEO, 9300 West Pico Blvd., Los Angeles, CA 90035, (800) 824-6109. Ron Levanson, president; Rana Arons, VP acquisitions.Home video features, how-to, sports.

AMERICAN HOME VIDEO LIBRARY, 1500 Broadway, Suite 1807, New York, NY 10136, (212) 869-2616, Marc Chase Weinstein, programming and marketing. How-to, travel, health and children's programs.

ASTRALVISION COMMUNICATIONS, 8949 Sunset Blvd., Los Angeles, CA 90096, (213) 275-5429. Jon Edwards. Video art, music concerts. Produces original programs.

BEST FILM AND VIDEO CORP, 98 Cutter Mills Rd., Great Neck, NY 11021, (516) 487-4515. Roy B. Winnick, president. Home video.

BFA EDUCATIONAL MEDIA, 468 Park Ave. S., New York, NY

10016, (212) 684-5910. H. Gelles, president. A division of Phoenix Films. Cultural, educational, children's, entertainment.

BLACKHAWK FILMS, 1235 W. 5th St., Davenport, IA 52808, (319) 323-9736, Ted Edwing. Vintage movies, shorts, cartoons, religious, documentaries, how-tos.

BOOK OF THE MONTH CLUB, INC., 485 Lexington Ave., New York, NY 10017, (212) 867-4300. George Spitzer, director. How-to, children's.

BOOKSHELF VIDEO, 301-B W. Dyer Rd., Santa Ana, CA 92707, (714) 957-0206. Mike Kahled, president. How-to, sports, cultural, entertainment.

BUDGET VIDEO, 1540 N. Highland Ave., Los Angeles, CA 90028, (213) 466-2431. Larry S. Fine. Classics, documentaries, foreign films, shorts, cartoons, sports, and children's programs.

CARAVATT COMMUNICATIONS INC., 551 Fifth Ave., New York, NY 10176, (212) 986-2005. Specialty home video marketing organization. How-tos.

CASTELLI-SONNABEND GALLERY, 420 W. Broadway, New York, NY 10012. Art films, experimental, videotapes.

CBS VIDEO CLUB/CBS VIDEO LIBRARY, (Subs. of Columbia House), 1400 N. Fruitridge Ave., Terre Haute, IN 47811, and 1211 Avenue of the Americas, New York, NY 10036, (212) 975-4875. Harry Eliaf, VP new business development. Distributes product of other video manufacturers.

CBS/FOX VIDEO, 1211 6th Ave., New York, NY 10036, (212) 819-3200, Todd P. Leavitt, senior VP of programming and business affairs; Mitch Horwitz, vp, programming and acquisition. The largest home video distributor. Recent films and classics, documentaries, shorts, cartoons, sports, religion, how-to, children's programs, music.

CHILDREN'S VIDEO LIBRARY (CVL), 60 Long Ridge Rd., P.O. Box 4000, Stamford, CT 06907, (203) 968-0000. A division of Vestron Video. C. J. Kettler, vice president; Angela Cifone, acquisitions. Major distributor of children's programming. Producer of original children's programs.

CHRONICLE VIDEO CASSETTES, 9000 Sunset Blvd., Suite 415, Los Angeles, CA 90069, (213) 858-0141. Bill Hickey, president. How-to, sports, arts, children's, educational, music, entertainment.

CHURCHILL FILMS, 622 North Robertson Blvd., Los Angeles, CA 90069, (213) 657-5110. George McQuilkin, president. Educational, children's, medical, science.

COLISEUM VIDEO, 430 W. 54th St., New York, NY 10019, (212) 489-8130. Produces original wrestling home video programs. Jerry Smallwood, director of marketing.

CORINTH VIDEO, 410 E. 62nd Street, New York, NY 10021, (212) 421-4770. Matthew Curtis. Features, documentaries, shorts, non-theatrical educational and entertainment programs.

COVENANT VIDEO, 3200 W. Foster Ave., Chicago, IL 60625, (800) 621-1290. Ted Ericson, programming; Deborah Lundberg, marketing. Religious programs, documentaries and children's shows. Mostly original productions. Mail order, Christian bookstores.

CROWN VIDEO, 1 Park Ave., New York, NY 10016, (212) 532-9200.

DIRECT CINEMA LIMITED, Box 69589, Los Angeles, CA 90069, (213) 656-4700. Mitchell W. Block. Documentaries, narrative films, non-theatrical.

DISCOUNT VIDEO TAPES, 3711 Clark Ave., Suite B, Burbank, CA 91521, (818) 843-3366. Woody Wise, president. Vintage movies and TV shows, documentaries and cartoons.

DISNEY HOME VIDEO, 500 S. Buena Vista St., Burbank, CA 91521, (818) 840-1000. Ben Tenn, VP of Retail Products. Major movies, cartoons, documentaries, family features, children's programs and wildlife.

EMBASSY HOME ENTERTAINMENT, 1901 Avenue of the Stars, Los Angeles, CA 90067, (213) 553-3600. Robert Blay, VP acquisitions; Diane McGee-Terry, manager special events; Al Eicher, programming. Recent films, TV shows, children's shows, health, music concerts. Video discs. Retail, international.

FAITH FOR TODAY, 1100 Rancho Conejo Blvd., Newbury Park, CA 91320, (805) 499-4363. Donald James. Religious shows, health, and documentaries.Mail order and retail, Japan and Australia.

FAMILY HOME ENTERTAINMENT, 21800 Burbank Blvd., Woodland Hills, CA 91365, (800) 423-7455. Kricket Wertz, director of acquisitions. Children's shows, shorts, concerts.

HARMONY VISION, 116 N. Robertson Blvd., Suite 701, Los Angeles, CA 90048, (213) 652-8844. Jerry Percell, president. Music, entertainment.

INCREASE VIDEO, 8265 Sunset Blvd., Suite 105, Hollywood, CA 90046, (213) 654-8808.

INDEPENDENT UNITED DISTRIBUTORS (IUD), 430 W. 54th St., New York, NY 10019, (800) 223-0313.

IRS VIDEO, 633 N. La Brea, Los Angeles, CA 90036, (818) 508-1657. Music videos.

INTERNATIONAL VIDEO ENTERTAINMENT (IVE), 7920 Alabama Ave., Canoga Park, CA 91304-4991, (800) 423-7455. Len Levy, senior vice president. Family fare, horror genre.

KARL/LORIMAR HOME VIDEO, 3970 Overland Ave., Suite 205, Culver City, CA 90230, (213) 280-0190. Stuart Karl, president; Lee Mandell, vp, acquisitions; Steve Burnstein, vp, acquisitions; Sydney Levine, acquisitions. Children's shows, sports, documentaries, how-tos, exercise, original home video programs.

KARTES VIDEO, 10 E. 106th St., Indianapolis, IN 46280, (317) 844-7403. Jim Kartes, president; C. B Wismar, director of acquisitions. Classics, features, how-to, original programs.

KID TIME VIDEO, 2340 Sawtelle Blvd., Los Angeles, CA 90064, (213) 452-9006. Children's video programs.

KULTUR, 121 Highway #36, West Long Branch, NJ 07764, (201) 842-6693. Dennis Hedlund, president. Cultural home video programming.

LIGHTNING VIDEO, 60 Long Ridge Rd., Stamford, CT 06905, (203) 968-0000. Gordon Bossin, vp marketing; Ruth Vitale, senior vp film programming; Larry Kassanoff, vp feature films; Michael Wiese, vp original programs. Features, original programs, travel.

MALJACK PRODUCTIONS, 15825 Rob Roy Dr., Oak Forest, IL 60452, (800), 323 0442. Waleed Ali, president; Jaffer Ali. Films, docus, old TV shows on home video.

MCA HOME VIDEO, 100 Universal City Plaza, Universal City, CA 91608, (818) 777-4300. Gene Giaquinto, president; Ted Schmitt, senior vp programming; Sue Peterson, director of programming for original properties. Major motion pictures, vintage TV shows, music, sports, health, how-to, children's programs. Original productions.

MEDIA HOME ENTERTAINMENT, 5730 Buckingham Parkway,

Culver City, CA 90230, (800) 421-4509. Niki Marvin, director of acquisitions; Kathie Van Brunt, vp acqusitions. Features, original home video.

MGM/UA HOME VIDEO, 1350 Avenue of the Americas, New York, NY 10019, (212) 408-0600, (800) 468-7600. John Ruskin, vp programming; Stephanie Schulman, marketing. Features, classic films, original home video programs.

MONTEREY HOME VIDEO, 7920 Alabama Ave., Canoga Park, CA 91304, (818) 888-3040. Scott Mansfield, programming. Movies, music concerts, and health programs. Produces original programs. Mail order and retail.

MTI TELEPROGRAMS, 3710 Commercial Ave., Northbrook, IL 60062, (800) 323-5343. Lloyd Singer. Safety, health education. Distributes ABC's Wide World Catalog. Schools, colleges, corporations, government, hospitals and health care organizations.

NATIONAL AUDIOVISUAL CENTER (GSA), Washington, DC 20409, (301) 763-1881. John Constance. Government produced training and educational films and tapes for schools, corporations, libraries.

NEW AGE VIDEO INC., P.O. Box 669, Old Chelsea Station, New York, NY 10113, (212) 254-1482. Ted Klempner, sales rep. Educational, dance, music.

NEW DAY FILMS, 7 Harvard Square, Brookline, MA 02146, (617) 566-5914. Filmmaker's cooperative for independent films. Labor history, aging, alternative health care, women, social films. Run by filmmakers.

NEW WORLD VIDEO, 1888 Century Park E., Fifth Floor, Los Angeles, CA 90067, (213) 201-0741. Feature films and home video.

NFL FILMS, 330 Fellowship Rd., Mt. Laurel, NJ 08054, (609)

778-1600. Ed Sabol, president. NFL football and sports films/home video.

NIGHTINGALE-CONANT CORP., 3730 W. Devon Ave., Chicago, IL 60659, (312) 647-0300. Arnold Carter. Produces original how-to programs. Mail order and other distributors. Self-help, motivational.

NORSTAR VIDEO CORP., 1580 Old Bayshore Hwy., San Jose, CA 95112 (408) 280-0522. Mail order distributor of how-to and specialty programs.

NOSTALGIA MERCHANT, 6255 Sunset Blvd., Hollywood, CA 90028 (213) 216-7900. Deanne Olson. Movies, TV shows, cartoons, children's shows. A division of Media Home Entertainment.

PACIFIC ARTS VIDEO RECORDS, 50 La Cienega Blvd. Suite 210, Beverly Hills, CA 90211, (213) 657-2233. Peter Kliener, director of acquisitions. Movies, concerts, video art, music videos, and comedies. Produces original programs.

PARAMOUNT HOME VIDEO, 5555 Melrose Ave., Hollywood, CA 90038, (213) 468-5000. Bob Klingensmith; Tim Clott, general manager; Eric Doctorow, vp marketing; Henry Seggerman, director of production and acquisitions. Major motion pictures, entertainment, comedy, original programs.

PBS VIDEO, 475 L'Enfant Plaza SW, Washington, DC 20024, (800) 424-7963. Mark Stanislawski. Distribution of educational programs that have appeared on PBS to business, educational, cable markets.

PHOENIX FILMS/BFA EDUCATIONAL MEDIA, 468 Park Ave. South, New York, NY 10016, (212) 684-5910. H. Gelles, president. Shorts for educational and library markets, cultural, arts, entertainment.

PRISM, 1875 Century Park E., Suite 1010, Los Angeles, CA, 90067,

(213) 277-3270. Barry Collier, president; Mel Franks, director of acquisitions. Features, music, entertainment, childrens, romance.

PIONEER VIDEO, 200 West Grand Ave., Montvale, NJ 07645, (201) 573-1122. Ken Kai, president; Barry Shereck, programming. Music concerts and music videos. Laser disks.

PYRAMID FILM AND VIDEO, Box 1048, Santa Monica, CA 90406, (213) 828-7577. Lynn and David Adams, owners. Shorts for non-theatrical and library market, health, children's films, innovative shorts, business.

RANDOM HOUSE VIDEO, 201 E. 50th St., New York, NY 10022, (212) 751-2600. Ed Martin, Rob Singer, marketing. How-to, children's, educational.

RCA/COLUMBIA HOME VIDEO, 2901 W. Alameda Ave., Burbank, CA 91505, (818) 954-4950. Robert Blattner, president; Gary Khammar, senior vp programming; Larry Estes, director, acquisitions. Movies, shorts, music concerts, children's programs.

RHINO VIDEO, 1201 Olympic Blvd., Santa Monica, CA 90404, (213) 450-6323. Randi Freeman, president. Compilations, comedy.

SONY VIDEO SOFTWARE, 1700 Broadway, New York, NY 10019, (212) 757-4990. John O'Donnell, president. Children's, arts, features, music videos.

SPINNAKER SOFTWARE, One Kendall Square, Cambridge, MA 02139, (617) 494-1200. Children's home video.

THORN EMI/HBO VIDEO INC., 1370 Avenue of the Americas, New York, NY 10019, (212) 977-8990. Frank O'Connell, president; Cindy Anthony-Kimball, vp communications and marketing. Features, sports, HBO films, children's, classical music, cultural.

TIME-LIFE VIDEO, 1271 Avenue of the Americas, New York, NY

10020, (212) 484-5928. Jane Garvey. Science, literature, business training tapes for schools, college, business and government.

USA HOME VIDEO, 7920 Alabama Ave., Canoga Park, CA 91304, (213) 888-3040. Kricket Wertz, director programming. Movies, concerts, health. Videodisc. Mail order, retail, international. (Also see Family Home Entertainment.)

VESTRON VIDEO, 60 Long Ridge Road, PO Box 4000, Stamford, CT 06907, (203) 968-0000. Jon Peisinger, president; Ruth Vitale, senior vp film programming; Mitchell Cannold, vp, Vestron Pictures; Larry Kasanoff, vp, feature films; C. J. Kettler, vp, Children's Video Library; Michael Wiese, vp, Vestron MusicVideo and original program development/production. The largest independent home video distributor and producer of made-for-home-video programs; comedy, how-to, exercise, sports, documentaries, travel, cultural.

VIDAMERICA, 235 E. 55th St., New York, NY 10022, (212) 355-1600. Al Markim, programming; Gary Needle, marketing. Movies, children's programs, sports, health, and how-to. Original program production.

VIDEO CASSETTE MARKETING, 137 Eucalyptus Drive, El Segundo, CA, 90245, Jim Spencer, president. How-to, exercise, documentaries.

VIDEODISC PUBLISHING INC., 381 Park Ave. S., Suite 1601, New York, NY 10016, (212) 685-5522. Steve Sagman, marketing manager. Disc only of cultural, arts, educational and entertainment programs.

VIDEO GEMS, 731 N. LaBrea Avenue, Los Angeles, CA 90038, (800) 421-3252, (213) 938-2385. Joseph Infante, president. Films, documentaries, health, how-to, sports, and children's programs. Retail.

VIDEO NATURALS, 2590 Glen Green, Suite #6, Los Angeles, CA

90068. Steven Siporin, president. Environmental, mood and relaxation videos.

VIDEO SCHOOL HOUSE, Sallyforth Video, 2611 Garden Road, Monterey, CA 93940, (408) 375-4474, (800) 345-1441 in Ca., outside Ca., (800) 367-0432. Sally Lasater, president. Large mail order catalog of specialty and alternative programs.

VIDEO YESTERYEAR, P.O. Box C, Sandy Hook, CT 06482, (203) 426-2574. Jonathon Sonnenborn. Movies, children's shows, concerts, cartoons and old TV shows.

VIDEOTAKES, 220 Shrewsbury Avenue, Red Bank, NJ 07701, (201) 747-2444. Joe Kennedy, president; Jenny Peters, director of programming. Large mail order catalog of sports, travel, entertainment, and specialty titles.

VIDEOTAPE CATALOG, SMW Video, Inc., 803 Russell Blvd., No. 2, Davis, CA 95616, (800) 547-0653. Morlee Griswold, president. Large mail order catalog of travel, cooking, fitness, music, dance, how-to, self-improvement and specialty programs.

WARNER HOME VIDEO, 4000 Warner Blvd, Burbank, CA 91522, (818) 954-6000. Warren Lieberfarb, president; Elyse Eisenberg, director, feature film acquisition; Barbara O'Sullivan, vp marketing. Major movies, cartoons, documentaries, exercise, how-to, and children's programs. Distributes Hardware Wars.

WIZARD VIDEO/FORCE VIDEO, 1551 N. LaBrea Ave., Los Angeles, CA 90028, (213) 850-6563. Charles Band, president. Exploitation sci-fi and horror films.

XEROX INFORMATION RESOURCES GROUP/PUBLISHING, One Pickwick Plaza, PO Box 6710, Greenwich, CT 06836, (203) 625-5675.

SOME DUPLICATORS

Allied Film and Video, Chicago, IL, (312) 348-0373

Allied Film and Video, Detroit, MI, (313) 871-2222

All Mobile Video, New York, NY, (212) 757-8919

C & C Visual, New York, NY, (212) 684-3830

Capitol Video Communications, Washington, DC, (202) 965-7800

Century III Teleproduction, Boston, MA, (617) 267-6400

Communications Concepts, Cape Canaveral FL, (305) 783-5232

Creative Video Services, St. Cloud, MN, (612) 255-0033

Dallas Post-Production Center, Irving TX, (214) 556-1043

Devlin Productions, New York, NY, (212) 582-5572

Editel/Chicago, Chicago, IL, (312) 440-2360

Editel/Los Angeles, Los Angeles, CA, (213) 931-1821

Editel/New York, New York, NY, (212) 867-4600

First Communications, Atlanta GA, (404) 980-9773

Image Transform, North Hollywood, CA, (818) 985-7566

Innovision Teleproduction, Lawrence, KS, (913) 843-9148

Interface Video Systems, Washington, DC, (202) 861-0500

International Production Center, New York, NY, (212) 582-6530

Koplar Communications Center, St Louis, MO, (314) 454-6324

Media Associates, Mt. View, CA, (415) 968-2444

Midtown Video, Denver, CO, (303) 778-1681

MTI, New York, NY, (212) 355-0510

Northwest Teleproductions, Kansas City, MO, (816) 531-3838

Northwest Teleproductions, Minneapolis, MN, (612) 835-4455

PCA Teleproductions, Matthews, NC, (704) 847-8011

Polycom Teleproductions, Chicago IL, (312) 337-6000

Skaggs Telecommunications, Salt Lake City, UT, (801) 539-1427

Southwest Teleproductions, Dallas, TX, (214) 243-5719

Telemation Productions, Seattle, WA, (206) 623-5934

Third Coast Video, Austin, TX, (512) 473-2020

VCA/Technicolor, Des Plaines, IL, (312) 298-7700

Versatile Video, Sunnyvale, CA, (408) 734-5550

BIBLIOGRAPHY

PRODUCTION

Video Editing and Post-Production: A Professional Guide, Knowledge Industry Publications, 701 Westchester Ave, White Plains, NY 10604.

New York Feature Film and Video Guide, 90 Riverside Drive, New York, NY 10024, $5.

Professional Video Production, by Ingrid Weigand, Knowledge Industry Publications, (see above), 1985.

Television Production, Alan Wurtzel, McGraw-Hill, New York, NY, 1983.

Television Production Handbook, by Herbert Zettl, Wadsworth Publishing Company, Belmont, CA, 1984.

The Video Production Guide, by Lon McQuillin, Howard Sams Publishing, Indianaoplis, IN, 1983.

Motion Picture, TV and Theater Directory, $4.25, Motion Picture Enterprises, Tarrytown, NY 10591.

DISTRIBUTION

The Independent Film and Videomakers Guide, by Michael Wiese, Revised and Expanded 1986, Michael Wiese, PO Box 406, Westport, CT 06881, $16.70 post-paid.

Doing it Yourself: A Handbook on Independent Film Distribution by

The Association of Independent Video and Filmmakers Inc., and written by Julia Reichert, 99 Prince Street, New York, NY 10012, 1977.

Making Films Your Business by Mollie Gregory, $6.95, Schocken Books, New York, 1979.

The Film Industries; Practical Business and Legal Problems in Production, Distribution and Exhibition, by Michael F. Mayer, $11.50, Hastings House, 1978.

Motion Picture Distribution-Business or Racket?, by Walter E. Hurst and Wm. Storm Hale, Seven Arts, Hollywood, 1975.

16mm Distribution by Judith Trojan & Nadine Covert, $6, available from Educational Film Library Association, 43 West 61st Street, New York, NY 10023.

Distribution Guide by The Independent Film Journal, 1251 Avenue of the Americas, New York, NY.

Producing, Financing and Distributing Film, by Farber and Baumgarten, Drama Book Specialists, New York, NY, 1973.

BUDGETS

Film and Video Budgets, by Michael Wiese, PO Box 406, Westport, CT 06881, (203) 226-6979, (1986), $14.95 plus $1.75 shipping. A line-by-line examination of a wide range of budgets for productions in both film and video formats. Includes student films, shorts, documentaries, commercials, pay cable segments, location and studio productions. Special sections on negotiations, money-saving tips and production procedures.

Film Scheduling, $16.95, Film Scheduling/Film Budgeting Workbook, $15.95, Movie Production and Budget Forms...Instantly!, by Ralph S. Singleton, $15.95 from Lone Eagle Publishing, 9903 Santa Monica Blvd., Beverly Hills, CA 90212.

The Hollywood Guide to Film Budgeting and Script Breakdown, by Danford Chamness, 1977, $20, from Stanley J. Brooks Company, 1460 Westwood Blvd., Suite 201, Los Angeles, CA 90024, (213) 470-2849. Demonstrates how to breakdown a script for the production board to estimate budgets for feature films.

1983-1984 Brooks' Standard Rate Book, $23, available from Stanley J. Brooks Co., (see above). Union and guild technicians wages for budgeting features.

Production Boards and Strips: For Features and Television, Stanley J. Brooks Co. (see above). Showing a day-by-day, scene-by-scene, filming of a feature.

1986 Motion Picture Almanac & Television Almanac (2 books), from Quigley Publishing Company, 159 West 53rd Street, NY, New York 10019. A complete listing of the feature film and television industries including producers, directors, stars, literary agents, distributors, press lists, up-to-date studio personnel, ad agencies, television stations and theater chains.

The Movie Business: American Film Industry Practice, by Wm. Bluem and Jason Squire, Hastings House, New York, 1972.

TRADE PUBLICATIONS

American Cinematographer, 220 E. 42nd St., Suite 930, New York, NY 10017, $15.95 per year.

Backstage, 5151 Wilshire Blvd., Suite 302, Los Angeles, CA 90036, $35 per year.

Billboard, 1515 Broadway, New York, NY 10036, $148 per year.

Hollywood Reporter, 6715 Sunset Blvd, Hollywood, CA 90028, $89 per year.

Millimeter, 826 Broadway, New York, NY 10003, $40 per year.

The Producer's Masterguide, New York Production Manual, Inc, 611 Broadway, Suite 807, New York, NY 10012, $69.95 per year.

Rockamerica Magazine, 27 E. 21st St. New York, NY 10010, $3.50 per issue.

Television Digest, 475 5th Ave., Suite 1021, New York, NY 10017.

Variety, (Weekly) also comes as a daily, from Variety, Inc, 154 W. 46th St. New York, NY 10036, $75 per year.

View: The Magazine of Cable TV Programming, $36/year, Subscription Services Dept., PO Box 5011, FDR Station, New York, NY 10022.

HOME VIDEO

American Video Trade Weekly, 8265 Sunset Blvd., Los Angeles, CA 90046.

Home Video Marketplace, and Home Video Report, Knowledge Industry Publications, 701 Westchester Ave., White Plains, NY 10604.

Home Viewer Magazine, 11 N. 2nd St., Phildelphia, PA 19106.

The Videocassette Recorder: An American Love Affair, Book Order Desk, Television Digest, Inc, 1836 Jefferson Place, N.W., Washington, DC 20036, 1985, $95.

The Video Source Book, National Video Clearinghouse, 100 Lafayette Dr., Syosset, NY 11791, $149 plus $5 shipping.

Videography, 475 Park Ave. S., New York, NY 10016, $15 per year.

Video, 460 W. 34th St., New York, NY 10001, $18 per year.

Video Advisor News, 2457 S. 133rd, Seattle, WA 98168.

Video Business, 135 W. 50th St., New York, NY 10020.

Video Insider, 223 Conestoga Rd., Wayne, PA 19087.

Video Industry Profile, 1775 Broadway, 7th Fl., New York, NY 10019.

Video Movies, 3841 W. Oakton St, Skokie, IL 60076, $26.40 per year.

Video Magazine, 460 W. 34th St., New York, NY 10001.

Video Music Magazine, 475 Park Ave. S., New York, NY 10016.

The Video Register (Annual), Knowledge Industry Publications, 701 Westchester Ave., White Plains, NY 10604, $59.50.

Home Video Publisher, Knowledge Industry Publishing, (see above), $225 per year.

The VCR Letter, Paul Kagan Associates, Inc., 126 Clock Tower Place, Carmel, CA 93923-8734.

Video Review Magazine, Viare Publishing, 902 Broadway, New York, NY 10010, $9.95 per year.

Video Marketing Newsletter, Suite 820, 1680 Vine St., Hollywood, CA 90028.

Video Week, Television Digest, 1836 Jefferson Place, N.W., Washington, DC 20036, $442 per year.

Video Times, Publications International, 3841 W. Oakden St, Skokie, IL 60076, $19.95 per year.

FEATURES

Independent Feature Project/Conference Packet, $25, has lists of foreign TV and theatrical buyers, distributors and exhibitors willing to screen independent feature films, from Independent Feature Project, 80 East 11th Street, New York, NY 10003.

Nuts and Bolts, Producing the Independent Feature Film, 1983, a transcript of a seminar held at the Variety Arts Center in Los Angeles from The Independent Feature Project/West, 309 Santa Monica Blvd., Room 422, Santa Monica, CA 90401, (213) 451-8075.

Low Budget Features by William Brown, $20, Los Angeles on budgeting low budget features.

The Movie Business Book, edited by Jason E. Squire, 1983, $13.95, Prentice-Hall, Inc., Englewood Cliffs, NJ, 07632.

Independent Feature Film Production, by Gregory Goodell, 1982, $17.95, St Martin's Press, 175 Fifth Ave., New York, NY 10010.

WRITING/CREATIVE

Screenplay, The Foundations of Screenwriting, by Syd Field, $4.95, Delacorte, 1982, New York.

The Screenwriter's Workbook, by Syd Field, Dell Publishing, 1 Dag Hammarskjold Plaza, New York, NY 10017, 1984.

A Whack on the Side of the Head: How to Unlock Your Mind for Innovation, by Roger von Oech, Ph. D., Warner Books, 666 Fifth Avenue, New York, NY 10103, 1983, $8.95. Ways to increase your creativity.

Drawing on the Right Side of the Brain, by Betty Edwards, Tarcher Publishing, 9110 Sunset Blvd, Los Angeles, CA 90069, $9.95. A course in enhancing creativity and artistic confidence.

The Art of Creative Writing and The Art of Dramatic Writing by Lajos Egri, $3.95, Citadel Books.

ASSOCIATIONS

Academy of Home Video Arts and Sciences, 1370 Ave. of the Americas, New York, NY 10019.

American Video Association, 557 E. Juanita Ave., Suite 3, Mesa, AZ 85204.

Association of Independent Video and Filmmakers, 625 Broadway, New York, NY 10012.

International Tape/Disc Association, 10 Columbus Circle, Room 2270, New York, NY 10019.

National Association of Television Program Executives, 342 Madison Ave., Suite 933, New York, NY 10173.

National Association of Video Distributors, 1255 23rd St., N.W., Washington, DC 20037.

Video Software Dealers Association (VSDA), 1008-F Astoria Blvd., Cherry Hill, NJ 08003.

Videotape Production Assocation, 565 5th Ave., Suite 416, New York, NY 10017.

THE INDEPENDENT FILM AND VIDEOMAKERS GUIDE

$14.95, ISBN 0-941188-03-5

This newly revised edition for 1986 provides a nuts-and-bolts approach to the production and distribution of an independent film. Wiese gets right to the heart of the matter by concentrating on the practicalities of finding investors, preparing the prospectus, researching the market, and arranging distribution contracts.

Includes Special
Sections on:

- Financing Your Film/Tape
- Investor Presentations
- Writing A Prospectus
- Market Research
- Finding Distributors
- Pay TV Program Buyers
- Music Videos

"Highly recommended . . . Wiese writes well, a highly personal book. No other book like this one has appeared on the market."

Choice Magazine

"Professionals will find that Mr. Wiese has a very clear idea of the problems facing the independent media artist and creative and practical solutions to offer."

WAFVL,
Washington, DC

FILM AND VIDEO BUDGETS

$14.95, ISBN 0-941188-02-7

A practical, comprehensive book that brings together advice on budgeting for a wide variety of film and video projects. Readers can look up sample budgets similar to their own and find a wealth of information on costs and savings.

An invaluable resource for anyone involved in producing low budget features, documentaries, commercials or music videos. No other book of this kind exists in the market.

Covers How To Prepare
Budgets For:

- Documentaries
- Commercials
- Shorts
- Music Videos
- Low Budget Features
- Film-To-Tape
- Student Films
- Pay TV Segments

Includes Special
Sections On:

- Money-Saving Tips
- Accounting
- Computer Budgets
- Negotiations
- Line Items
- Guild Contacts

HOME VIDEO: PRODUCING FOR THE HOME MARKET

$16.95, ISBN 0-941188-04-3

The first book of its kind to bring together comprehensive information and clear advice on the successful development and distribution of original home video programs. Genres such as comedy, how-to, documentaries, children, sponsored and music videos are discussed in detail. The book examines new marketing opportunities for independent producers. There are valuable insights on presentations, co-productions, budgeting, negotiation of contracts, and creative marketing.

Includes Special
Sections on:

- Developing Ideas
- Pitching Projects
- Program Genres
- Marketing Ideas
- Financing
- Video Budgets
- Contracts
- Packaging

Up-to-date, valuable information for anyone who is producing for the home video marketplace.

Order Form

MICHAEL WIESE
PO Box 406
Westport, CT 06881
Telephone (203) 226-6979

I am enclosing $ __________ . Please send the following books:

_____ ***The Independent Film and Videomakers Guide,*** $14.95
_____ ***Film and Video Budgets,*** $14.95
_____ ***Home Video: Producing for the Home Market,*** $16.95

Name ____

Address ____

City/State/Zip _______________________________________

Please add sales tax of 7.5% for books shipped to Connecticut addresses. (1.12, $1.27).

Shipping: Add $1.75 first book.
Add $1.50 second book.
Add $1.00 each additional book.

Foreign Orders: Add $3.00 each, sea mail.
Add $6.00 each, air mail.

Discount of 30% for total order of 5 books or more.